THE
BALLOON
BOOK

D0578273

By the same author

BASIC GUIDE TO FLYING

THE COMPLETE GUIDE TO CANOEING AND KAYAKING

Original painting by Barclay Ferguson.

THE BALLOON BOOK

by PAUL FILLINGHAM

Including:

- *101 questions and answers about ballooning*

- *a comprehensive balloon flight training guide*

- *a fascinating history of ballooning through the ages*

DAVID McKAY COMPANY, INC.
New York

Library of Congress Cataloging in Publication Data

Fillingham, Paul.
　The balloon book.

　Bibliography: p.
　Includes index.
　1. Balloons.　　I. Title.
TL610.F5　　　797.5　　　76-41056
ISBN　0-679-50594-6

Designed by Jacques Chazaud

MANUFACTURED IN THE UNITED STATES OF AMERICA

Line drawings by Judith Mitchell

Photo Credits: Paul Fillingham, pages 44, 45, 47,
48, 60, 62, 63, 65, 66, 79, 80, 87; New York
Public Library Picture Collection, pages 5, 6, 29,
31, 122, 124, 125, 127, 128, 129, 155, 156, 158;
Yale Joel, page 34; Jerry Rose Studio, pages 35,
85, 196, 197; Goodyear Aerospace Corporation,
pages 171, 172; Alan C. Ross, page 185; Library
of Congress Picture Collection, pages 37, 143,
157, 159, 161, 166 bottom; The National Archives,
pages 4, 144, 145, 148, 149, 150, 151, 152, 163,
164, 165, 166 top, 167, 170.

For Joanne—and Renee, Larry and Nancy.
And in respectful memory of Fr. Francisco de Lana, whose ideas
and theoretically feasible attempts at lighter-than-air flight
in 1670 got the rest of us started.

Contents

"I have long been of the opinion . . . that the fields of air are open to knowledge, and that only ignorance and idleness need crawl upon the ground."

Samuel Johnson, 1759

PART I:

For the

Beginner

Introduction

*O*nce the Wright brothers had successfully shown that their motorized gliding machine could safely fly and that it had successfully demonstrated a passing dexterity of maneuver, most people were willing to trade in their aerostats (balloons) and soaring machines for the hottest thing in town—powered flight.

A few afficionados stayed with their balloons and dirigibles, since for quite some time in those early days, such aircraft as the Zeppelin were able to perform better and more grandly those tasks now relegated to fixed-wing aircraft. Indeed, some people still feel that airships performed much too efficiently (and economically) the peaceful task of moving people around the planet.

It was clear, however, that for military purposes fixed-wing machinery was less vulnerable to attack, though very valuable service was provided by blimps which guarded convoys in both world wars, and provided aerial defense.

The demise of the airship was slow but sure. Apart from the misfortunes of the U.S. Navy's *Shenandoah, Akron* and *Macon,* elsewhere the British R-101 and finally the *Hindenburg* met their fate. The R-101 was apparently the victim of shoddy workmanship, and many now consider the *Hindenburg* explosion to have been sabotage.

Still, a number of enthusiasts and a few scientists stayed with balloons, and stratospheric exploration became the next game. Starting in the 1930s the world's altitude record seesawed between the United States and the USSR, and though there were a few flights across the Alps each year, not too much ballooning was done.

But among pilots and a number of scientists there remained the impression that perhaps airships (and, indeed, balloons) were still somewhat ahead of their time. The feeling was that airships especially had been

The British R–100 seen here during trials worked fine but fell victim to decisions favoring . . .

. . . the ill-fated R–101, seen overflying Ludgate Hill by St. Paul's Cathedral in London, England.

France and Switzerland have active balloon pilots, and flights in the Alps occur annually. Aerostat here is a gas balloon.

invented fifty years ahead of the technology that could make them a safe as well as a practical means of transportation.

This consensus persisted following the Second World War, and in 1951 in Britain, Lord Ventry built a small 50,000-cubic-foot nonrigid with its envelope adapted from an observation balloon. It was fitted with a four-place gondola and a small 76-horsepower engine which provided a cruise speed of 30–35 miles per hour. In the United States, Goodyear production was minimal.

Then in 1961, as a result of a small U.S. Navy contract, the hot-air balloon was reborn. Dismissed as too dangerous in the years gone by—for fire was an ever-present risk—the hot-air balloon returned to service as a cheap, safe alternative to the increasingly expensive gas balloon, thanks to the application of modern technology. Within a few years, several new designs were to emerge in both the United States and Britain.

By the beginning of the 1970s, the sport warranted its own magazine in this country. Sales of hot-air balloons rose from a handful in 1966 to nearly 1,000 in 1975. That may not seem very significant, but when one

Hot-air balloons provide inexpensive flying.

considers the large number of people peripherally involved in the sport, that figure looks better. Experts predict that within the next five years these numbers are likely to triple, since ballooning has made great strides despite the faltering economy of recent years. It seems probable then, that ballooning is beginning a growth trend unparalleled in general aviation since the early 1960s saw the regeneration of private airplanes.

Much of the appeal of ballooning is that it is inexpensive (once you've purchased your gear or joined a club, and gotten that license). More important, it is the least regulated and most fun area of aviation today.

The big-business approach to private flying of recent years and the growth of the Federal Aviation Administration (FAA) bureaucracy have resulted in the dropout of several hundred thousand pilots—all bored with the increasing hassle, the burgeoning military-style regulation of the skies and the ever-increasing cost of ancillary equipment required to take an aircraft aloft.

Ballooning, the oldest form of flight, remains the last haven of those who would like to experience their sky in peace. And the modern hot-air or Montgolfier-type balloon allows them to do this in considerable safety and comfort—something that's still not readily available to those who enjoy that other increasingly popular skysport of hang-gliding.

This book, then, is about aerostation (ballooning). Unlike any of the other books on the subject, a complete flight-training briefing has been included. While the slant is toward the hot-air balloon—since this type of aerostat is so much cheaper than the gas balloon (Charliers type), the essential differences between the two are discussed. The basic principles remain the same, since both types depend upon the amount of lift they possess at the start of a flight. The gas balloon depends on its lighter-than-air gas which leaks away into the surrounding atmosphere, thus reducing its lift. The hot-air balloon depends on the gas it can burn to heat the air in its envelope, and as the fuel supply runs out, so the time left aloft is reduced.

Since many who are interested in the art of aerostation (it is an art rather than a science, which may be one of the reasons the FAA bureaucrats hesitate to interfere with it too seriously) may not be familiar with the essentials, the book opens with 101 questions and answers about the subject. This chapter might be called a background briefing; it attempts to put in perspective those items that most people want to know about before delving deeper into the subject.

Part II deals with the work involved in obtaining a license. Ballooning is not difficult, and provided you have an average amount of common sense, it's about as easy to learn as riding a bicycle. Nevertheless, there are FAA regulations on the subject that you are expected to know. (If the FAA were to insist on a private pilot's license as a test of merit before entering their employment, it is likely there would be considerably less regulation and fewer bureaucrats and greater safety in the skies than at present.) So Part II deals with paper pushing for the most part—you have to know it, and I've tried to make it as easy to understand as possible.

Part III deals with weather and navigation. The weather is important, and being your own weather forecaster makes it so much easier to enjoy ballooning. Even TV forecasts are not foolproof, and while they may be generally satisfactory, your own additional knowledge can upgrade their information.

Navigation may seem like a strange subject to include in a book about a sport in which you travel where the wind blows. But navigation is useful, since it tells you where you are, and if used in conjunction with your weather information, it allows you to adjust your course or change direction from time to time. For example, there is generally a tendency for the wind to shift in a clockwise direction as one ascends in the northern hemisphere. A southerly wind at the surface will usually become sou'westerly at about 3,000 feet above ground level (AGL). A northerly will move to nor'easterly given the same altitude differential. This is not a hard and fast rule, since different atmospheric conditions often give different results, but weather and navigation are important subjects for the aspiring aeronaut.

There's a look at radios, too, and their role in navigation. Since the FAA has virtually gotten into the business of selling radios to pilots,* they like you to know about radios, even though most balloonists don't bother with them except for competition or for record-breaking attempts. So in its written examination, the FAA still asks a number of questions about radios, which have scarcely any practical application for balloonists.

Part IV is background data on ballooning and contains a colorful history of the sport. It's a little different from most histories, since it includes information about several women balloonists whose exploits were often

---

* One of the ways a bureaucracy remains entrenched is by finding ways to help people make money by getting others to spend it. Over the past few years, the FAA has handed out a bounty to the people who make emergency locator transmitters (ELTs) by requiring all aviators to have them aboard their aircraft. Since that ukase, there have been innumerable problems with ELTs going off on their own and sending out false alarms, and ELTs which did not go off when they were needed. The FAA is now in the process of mandating other items of equipment, to the extent that many of the smallest light aircraft are currently equipping with avionics (special aircraft radios) which may cost as much as one third of the value of the aircraft in which they're installed.

overshadowed by those of their masculine counterparts. Like gliding, ballooning is eminently suitable as a woman's sport, since male ground crews can usually be relied on to do any heavy work involved.

Included here are some of the record breakers of the past, and a few of the more interesting practical applications of the art of aerostation. This section concludes with a brief look to the future, which will hopefully discover the potential of balloons as sky cargo ships. If their computerized tracks were to be traced across our heavens, the amount of pollution (both noise and gaseous) would be greatly reduced, as they would use much less fuel than the turgid metal giants that often warp our hearing.

For those interested in flight training, the appendices provide a list of the increasing number of schools as well as a listing of balloon makers and the various products they sell. There's a glossary of the more technical terms used in the book, and a bibliography and list of suggested reading to round it all out.

Ballooning is the sport for those who still feel most comfortable doing their own thinking. It is definitely for those who prefer to remain individuals in these times of conformity. For ballooning is certainly different. Its challenges are subtle and its rewards immeasurable.

In these times of the space shuttle and planetary system probes, aerostation still remains the true arcanum of flight. And to favored initiates it permits the veil of illusion to be drawn aside momentarily from the wearer's eyes.

Icarus fell. We don't have to.

But read on, and see why for yourself. And most important of all—enjoy!

101
Questions and Answers
About Ballooning

1. *How does a person get into ballooning?*

This depends on what kind of ballooning you want to do. Do you want to do it for business or pleasure? Do you want to compete? Or do you simply want to fly?

Whatever field of flying you think you're ready for, and no matter how enthusiastic you are to get started, the first thing you'll be told is: "Great! But first of all, take a ride, and then see whether you want to go any further."

2. *Okay. You decide to go for the ride. How much is that going to cost?*

A trial ride can cost from nothing to as much as $100; it depends on the establishment. And if you get a free ride the first time around, chances are if you continue with the sport, it'll show up on your account later on.

3. *Isn't $100 a bit expensive?*

If you compare the price to those five-dollar coupons some airplane manufacturers use to interest people in flying—sure. But don't forget that the price will probably also include some initial instruction with the balloon on a tethering line to the ground, so that you can get used to controlling ascent and descent input. Once you've got the hang of that—and you need not be very smart to catch on in about twenty minutes—you'll probably load up with fresh fuel and go cross-country (weather permitting) for about an hour or two.

4. *What other costs are involved?*

The person who is giving you the ride has overhead to pay. First, there's the commercial pilot who is going with you. While there are a whole lot of commercial pilots flying regular airplanes and helicopters, there simply aren't very many who are into ballooning.

Next, there's the instructor part of the deal. And while the commercial pilot can instruct, his time has to be paid for while he's instructing. There's also the truck and ground crew, usually three people; the equipment itself and insurance. Finally there's fuel cost. Despite the recent stupendous price hikes, there's no shortage of propane, which is regularly burned off, since it's cheaper for oil corporations to waste it than to build storage tanks which would keep the price down.

5. *What happens after you pay the initial fee?*

Since ballooning depends on the whims of the weather, you'll be told to meet the crew—wind and weather permitting—usually around dawn, since that's the best time for flying. Your introductory flight will take place, and then it's up to you to decide whether or not you want to go on. Very often a firm that charges money up front like this will apply your initial fee to the cost of a full training program, counting it as an introductory lesson.

6. *What are the chances of enjoying that first ride?*

Pretty good. The real thing will most likely make a believer of you. That introductory lesson or first flight is what you might call step two—if you haven't already attempted the art of aerostation.

7. *The art of what?*

Aerostation is a fancy word invented a long time ago for what we call ballooning. An aerostat is a balloon.

8. *And an aeronaut is a balloonist?*

You got that hole in one!

9. *How old are most balloonists?*

To be eligible for a student pilot certificate for a balloon or glider, a person must be at least fourteen years old, sixteen for a private pilot's license, and eighteen for a commercial pilot certificate. Devotees range in age from fourteen to people in their eighties.

10. *Can you smoke in a balloon?*

If you want to, and only in a hot-air or helium-gas balloon. Smoking in hydrogen or coal-gas balloons is discouraged, since you could blow yourself up in the ensuing explosion.

11. *Is it correct to assume that ballooning is most expensive in the beginning?*

You'd be absolutely right. You might even call it an initiation fee, though of all forms of aviation, ballooning remains the least expensive.

12. *Are there balloon clubs?*

Sure. Ballooning is inexpensive and will give you flying at as little as five dollars an hour if you belong to a regular club. (But one must first acquire the skills demanded by the government which supposedly holds the skies in trust for all of us.)

13. *How expensive are balloon clubs?*

Figure on around $900 to join a club. It's a lot less expensive than any other form of flight once you've joined, since basic costs are pretty nominal.

If you don't have the funds, some dealers will rent to you once you have demonstrated that you know how to fly. The prices vary.

14. *What bureaucratic procedures are required by the government to fly a balloon?*

You'll need to get a student license. They'd like you to take a medical, but it isn't required. In the course of your studies—a briefing is included in this book—you'll need to answer a Federal Aviation Administration (FAA) written examination, which is only a little more clever than a driving test. You will also need to complete the number of hours required to establish some sort of competence in the art of ballooning. (This is discussed in detail in Chapter 4.) Finally, you will be assessed by an FAA designated inspector who will let you know whether you are good enough to be allowed to become a pilot. The procedure is very similar to the medieval guild system, in which persons were first apprenticed, then permitted to go solo while still nominally under supervision, before being able to work for themselves.

15. *How much does a student license cost?*

It is free, and any FAA district office can issue one.

16. *How expensive is a pilot's license?*

The least expensive way of getting your pilot's license from scratch would be via ballooning or soaring. The basic license for power flight used to cost around $1,000. That's gone up, to around $1,250 if you're lucky, but usually more, due to inflated fuel costs.

17. *How much do balloons cost?*

The average modern hot-air balloon that carries three persons costs around $5,000, ready to go. An additional $1,000 is necessary to purchase the skills (flight lessons) and license to get off the ground. After that, costs for getting airborne each time—fuel, maintenance, etc.—are agreeably low. Rental costs vary, depending on the type of balloon, but usually run about fifty dollars per person per day. Only hang-gliding is cheaper, and with ballooning you aren't likely to break your neck.

18. *How much does the cheapest balloon cost?*

The least expensive balloon on the market is an import from England which sells for $3,877. It's a two-place balloon and has a maximum certified lift—that's payload in ordinary terms—of 919.8 pounds at sea level. The least expensive American-made balloon costs $4,295.

19. *Suppose I want something that'll carry more than two people?*

The least expensive three-place balloon costs just a little more—$4,595 —and includes everything you'll need to fly.

20. *What is the balloon material made of?*

A very closely knit nylon is commonly used, similar to the ripstop nylon used in making lightweight tents for backpacking and mountaineering. The weave weighs around two ounces a yard, an amount which is increased slightly by special treatment for heat and ultraviolet resistance. It is highly durable given a modicum of care, and—most important—well proven.

21. *What are the general types of balloons?*

There are basically two kinds of balloons: hot-air and gaseous.

Up and away in my beautiful balloon . . .

22. *How do hot-air balloons operate?*

Fueled by propane (or butane), air is heated by burning the gas through a special burner system. The envelope is usually composed of a specially treated man-made fiber, designed to resist the high temperatures involved in heating the air sufficiently to provide lift.

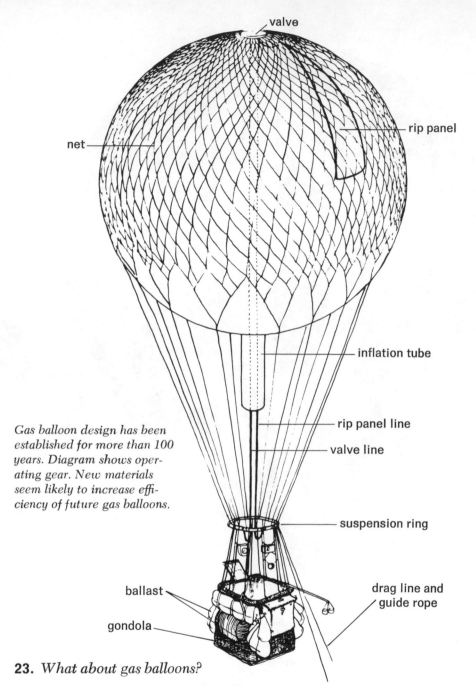

valve

rip panel

net

inflation tube

rip panel line

valve line

Gas balloon design has been established for more than 100 years. Diagram shows operating gear. New materials seem likely to increase efficiency of future gas balloons.

suspension ring

ballast

drag line and guide rope

gondola

23. *What about gas balloons?*

Gas balloons have always been at the expensive end of the scale. When ballooning was first discovered, in the late eighteenth century, it was the poorer people who figured out how you could fly using hot air. They had to give it a fancy name to get it accepted then, so they called it *phlogiston*, or essence of fire. The scientists of those days, whom the government supported—governments have always tended to support science and religion, since it adds to their credibility—were able to use hydrogen.

24. *Can we have a little less politics and more about balloons?*

Politics and ballooning have always been connected. Everyday people have always used hot-air balloons successfully. It's simply that when things become more costly, the majority are deprived of that enjoyment, as with gas balloons.

25. *Are balloonists rich?*

For the most part, definitely not. Many belong to clubs or form groups in order to share the costs. Balloonists generally include a cross section of socioeconomic strata.

26. *How are balloons classified?*

There is a relationship between volume and load in balloons, and this is measured by symbols. For example, an AX–5 balloon has a volume of slightly more than 40,000 cubic feet and can carry one or two people. An AX–6 at around 55,000 cubic feet will carry two to three people. An AX–7 at 70,000-plus cubic feet will carry three to four, depending on outside air temperature. These particular symbols apply to hot-air balloons.

27. *Haven't there been bigger balloons?*

Yes. There have been hot-air balloons with capacities of up to 500,000 cubic feet.

28. *Where can you go ballooning?*

You can fly a balloon from almost anywhere. For takeoff, a fairly large, clear space is nice. If it's windy, then a windbreak of trees is useful, but a backyard of a couple of acres is really all you need.

29. *Aren't there regulations about taking off in balloons?*

Yes. A balloon is, after all, a type of flying machine, and the FAA has a plenitude of rules and regulations to be followed by those who fly. These rules have to do with proficiency of the pilot and the rules of flight. (Like many other agencies in Washington, the FAA has become largely self-serving, an expanding empire builder that feeds on general aviation for the benefit of commercial airlines and the military.)

30. *What supporting gear do you need?*

An inflation fan is a great help in filling the balloon, though traditionalists prefer to flop cold air inside. Flopping air inside requires two persons who hold the throat of the envelope and literally "flop" cold air into it by moving it up and down. You may want a tether line if you're going to be practicing closely controlled ascents and descents.

31. *Exactly what is cold inflation?*

Cold inflation is to give you a chance to inspect the interior of the envelope and, at the same time, to reduce the chances of burning the fabric once the burners are lighted. A small fan is used to cold inflate, and is usually kept running, in order to mix and spread out the hot air, until hot-air inflation is completed. Most inflators run on a small, two-stroke gasoline engine.

32. *How long does it take to inflate a balloon?*

A hot-air balloon takes about fifteen minutes to inflate; a gas balloon usually a little longer.

33. *What about instruments?*

You'll use a compass to tell you in which direction you're traveling, an altimeter to tell you how high you are, a variometer—an instantaneous

Vertical Speed Indicator is a poor man's version of variometer, which is sensitive to up and down movement.

Altimeter is an aneroid barometer that instead of reading out changing air pressure provides the answer in feet or meters.

rate of climb/descent indicator—to tell you whether you're going up or down and at what speed, and a pyrometer which tells you how hot it is inside the top of the balloon. These instruments are all sold as part of the "package" when you buy a balloon.

34. *Is it important to know how hot it is up there?*

Yes. If you overheat the fabric you'll have to put a new panel in, since overheating weakens it. Modern fabrics are heat resistant, but too much heat for too long weakens them.

35. *How do you know if the fabric has had too much heat?*

If your pyrometer failed to work, you'd discover that the fabric had too much heat by noting the telltales, which are secured inside the top of the balloon, when you completed your walkaround inside prior to the next flight. The telltales are special pieces of material designed to change color (they go from white to black) after a certain amount of heat.

36. *As a matter of interest, how does one deflate?*

Most balloons have a special valve to permit deflation at the end of a flight. Hot-air balloons use a rip panel kept in place by Velcro fastenings, though other systems are also used.

37. *How long does it take for deflation?*

This also takes about fifteen minutes, which includes putting the envelope in its bag and getting everything stowed away in the gondola.

38. *What about the cockpit: What's the basket called?*

You can call it a basket, but it is usually referred to as a gondola or car.

39. *What is the gondola made of? And is it safe?*

It's certainly safe, unless you deliberately climb over the side. Today gondolas are made of fiberglass, or of aluminum tubing framework with either plywood or fiberglass panels. There are also traditional wicker gondolas, which are considered best because they are relatively light in weight, very strong, and energy absorbing—useful for rough landings. Wicker gondolas also enhance the beauty of a balloon, another reason why they are preferred.

Everyone gets to enjoy the fun with aerostation.

Troubles with other traffic don't worry the balloonist . . .

. . . as balloons take precedence over all other flying vehicles. Other traffic must give way.

40. *What happens if you meet an airplane while ballooning?*

Because balloons have only up-and-down control, all other air vehicles have to give them the right of way. (In the up-and-down regime, a balloon can be flown to an altitude more accurately than a helicopter—or as aeronauts would put it, "to the nearest foot.")

41. *How do you steer?*

Balloons have no directional steering device and make use of wind currents for their motion. By changing altitude, you can sometimes make useful changes in direction. But ballooning is more about flying itself than going to any particular place.

42. *Does it help to be able to fly an airplane if you want to fly a balloon?*

Experience in fixed-wing aircraft is useful only as far as overall flight experience is concerned. A balloon is a lighter-than-air vehicle, and a different set of rules applies to its operation, but you can use some of your fixed-wing flight time to make up the hours you require in obtaining your commercial license.

43. *Can you fly in poor weather, like rain or snow?*

If you don't mind getting wet and cold, yes, provided that visibility is reasonable and the rain is not too heavy.

44. *Can you fly at night?*

Yes, though most balloonists prefer to be in bed at night.

45. *Do you need to carry parachutes?*

Not as a rule, since you are unlikely to be doing aerobatics in a balloon. If the burner system goes out and you cannot ignite it, most modern balloons work like a parachute and bring you down at parachute speed. There are some balloonists who like to take parachutes with them, but these are probably people who also use belts *and* suspenders to keep their trousers up!

46. *Must you carry an anchor?*

These days balloonists don't bother with this, since landing procedures can be very precisely controlled, thanks to modern burner controls and venting systems.

47. *What about carrying sand?*

The modern hot-air balloonist has no need of ballast. Gas balloonists still use sand, since a gas balloon tends to lose its lift after a while, and the ballast will allow it to come down at an appropriate speed.

48. *Where is the fuel kept?*

The fuel is stored in lightweight aluminum tanks that are carried in the gondola. If you don't like to stand while you fly, you can usually perch on one of the fuel tanks.

49. *How much fuel should be carried?*

That depends on the size of the vehicle you're flying. The tanks usually contain twenty gallons of fuel. In a typical two- or three-place balloon, you'd carry two tanks, which would be sufficient for more than two hours of flight. Long-distance attempts require more. Malcolm Forbes, on his cross-country trip, carried up to sixteen containers, which he parachuted down when used, to be picked up by his back-up helicopter.

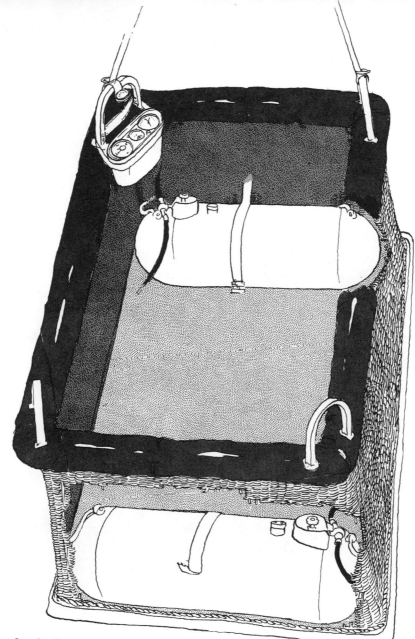

The wicker basket is favored for good strength-to-weight ratio plus cushion-effect in high-wind landings. Gas tanks are stowed out of the way. Small instrument panel is mounted on basket's rim.

50. *Doesn't it get cold at high altitudes?*

Cool, not cold. You see, there's a lot of heat radiated down into the gondola from the throat of the balloon and from the burners. Malcolm Forbes said that he really didn't notice the cold even when crossing the Rockies because of this effect.

51. *How fast can a balloon go up?*

Maximum rate of climb can be as much as 1,250 feet per minute, but normally you climb at a slower rate to conserve fuel.

52. *What about coming down?*

Again, you wouldn't want to come down too fast, so you usually maneuver at around five hundred feet per minute.

53. *Which is more difficult to fly: a hot-air or gas balloon?*

They're really about the same. In gas balloons you have to be careful about the ballast, while in hot-air balloons you have to watch the fuel and envelope temperature. Hot-air balloons are a little more complicated to fly because there are more controls. On the other hand, the additional controls make for more precision in all kinds of flight.

54. *What controls are there in a hot-air balloon?*

For ascent there's the burner, and for descent, the maneuvering vent—a special panel that can open and close and is used either to initiate a descent or to halt a climb. The ripping panel is used when you want to stop flying.

55. *After you've got the hang of ascents and descents, what else is there to learn?*

Go out and try it in the field—a cross-country flight in which you select a landing place, make an approach and descent, and then immediately take off again. This is exciting and requires skill, since unlike an airplane, the only control you have is the up/down—you can't steer.

56. *Is an approach made the same way as with an airplane?*

Yes. This is one advantage of being a regular pilot, since you will be familiar with the clues that perspective gives. For non-pilots this is the relationship that the ground and the horizon form when gliding in at a constant angle to a particular spot.

57. *Explain more about what happens once you decide to start flight training.*

Training is going to cost about $1,000 and you will require a minimum of seven to ten days to complete the program. These are simply ball-park figures; you can find cheaper prices in some parts of the country. The seven-to-ten-day time requirement is a standard minimum, however.

58. *If you have a regular pilot's license, can you expect a reduction?*

Not usually. As mentioned earlier, a balloon is a lighter-than-air vehicle, and this means learning a whole new way to fly. There's a different written exam to pass, whether or not you have an ordinary pilot's license. And the mode of operation of a balloon is in no way related to the safe operation of an airplane.

The only advantages you have as a pilot are that you are familiar with the fundamental rules of the game, general safety considerations, right-of-way rules and the Federal Aviation Regulations (FAR). That'll cut down your learning time—but not the fee.

59. *What do you need in order to get a private license for a balloon?*

A minimum of ten hours flying time, plus ground training, is required. Flight experience must include a flight to 3,000 feet Above Ground Level (AGL), plus two flights of at least thirty minutes duration each, and one solo flight. In addition, you will also have to fly a special test flight for your certification with an FAA-approved person.

60. *What is required for the commercial balloon license?*

Before you can get a commercial license you must have a private license. A total of thirty-five hours flying time as pilot is required. This includes twenty hours and ten flights in free balloons: six flights under the supervision of a commercial free balloon pilot, two solo flights, and two flights of at least sixty minutes each. Also required is one ascent under control to 5,000 feet AGL.

61. *Do you have to pay the total amount in advance?*

No. Normally you'll be asked for a basic deposit at the time you sign up, which may be up to one third of the total fee. You'll probably pay the remainder on an hourly basis. There are variations, and most training establishments make it as easy as possible for you.

62. *If you decide to buy your own balloon first, can you get a special rate to learn to fly?*

Sure, but expect to negotiate that first. You might expect to pay about a third less. It's not a big reduction, but as mentioned before, the people who provide sales and training are in business, as well as having fun, and there are overhead expenses involved. In a commercial outfit, these can be sizable.

63. *What about ground instruction?*

Apart from the standard rules and regulations, there's a certain amount of meteorology, basic weather forecasting, and some knowledge of wind patterns to be learned. There's also some physics—the hows and whys of balloons staying in the air, convection, radiation, and so forth. It's useful to know a bit about aircraft radios and how they work. The entire training program is geared to make you safe and responsible in operating your aerostat.

64. *How much does balloon insurance cost?*

Like almost all forms of insurance these days, far too much—the average cost is around $200 to $250 a year. A typical package from Lloyd's of London for business and pleasure, including passenger insurance, liability coverage and all-risk hull coverage, would run about $235. A commercial package permitting student flight training, balloon rental and any exhibitions, promotions or demonstration flights would run an additional $150. These rates are subject to change, however, and should be checked.

65. *How much liability coverage does one need?*

Normally you'd expect to have $300,000 liability, though you can get up to $1,000,000. However, as insurance underwriters discover that ballooning is very safe—and thus highly profitable business—rates will start to decline. This is already beginning to happen.

If you are running a commercial establishment then you must have insurance. You would want third-party liability coverage at the very minimum if you are a private flyer and would normally carry what is termed "hull" insurance for your balloon.

66. *How long will a balloon last?*

Given a minimum of attention, a balloon will last quite a number of years, and the gondola will last almost forever. Obviously, if you take care of the equipment, it'll last a lot longer. The first of the modern hot-air balloons, built in 1961, is still flying today.

67. *What can be done to make a balloon last?*

The two principle causes of wear and tear on balloons are (a) haphazard ground handling, causing holes either through tears from sharp objects or damage from careless inflation; and (b) in the air—not monitoring the temperature closely, causing excessive heat within the envelope, and carelessly hitting power lines. Finally, there's also leaving the fabric lying around when the sun is high in the sky. If you're flying at the time, there's not too much you can do about it, but if you're not flying, the envelope should be stowed out of the light.

68. *What happens if a balloon gets a hole in it?*

Small holes up to one square foot in size are of little consequence and simply cause you to use more fuel to compensate. On the other hand, it's inefficient to fly a balloon with holes in it, and they can be easily patched up.

69. *What happens if a bird flies into your balloon?*

Bird strikes are highly unusual, since the balloon is moving along at the same speed as the wind. Interested birds will sometimes fly by out of curiosity, but most prefer to keep their distance. If a bird does fly into the envelope, it will bounce off.

70. *How do you do a fabric test?*

A tensile-grab test and a pull-tear test are both used. If the fabric fails the test, new panels can be sewn in. If the envelope has been severely misused, you're better off getting a new one. Burners, gondolas and instruments will usually last forever. The skirt and throat are at the bottom of the envelope, and occasionally get burned from careless inflation.

71. *Is there an average envelope "life" in numbers of hours, like a regular aircraft or hull?*

Yes and no. The average "life" is three hundred to four hundred hours, but the figure is unproven in that there are so many variables, including pilot care.

72. *What about envelope maintenance? Do you send it back to the manufacturer?*

Yes, you can send it to the manufacturer, or to an FAA-approved repair station. A balloon is similar to an airplane in that you need to have a regular inspection. You are required to inspect the envelope and telltales at twenty-five-hour intervals and go over the material with a fine-tooth comb. This may mean changing valves and so on if necessary.

73. *Is there a 100-hour inspection?*

Yes. This is the same as an annual inspection. At the 100-hour point, the templates (telltales) are inspected very carefully to see whether the maximum internal temperatures have been exceeded. There are various other items which also have to be fully checked.

74. *How much responsibility does a student pilot have?*

As you progress you get more and more responsibility, but it all begins on the day when you conduct the initial walkaround, outside and inside, with your instructor.

75. *You walk around inside the balloon?*

Yes. The most important preflight check is the one made inside the balloon envelope when it is partially inflated with cold air. The ripping panel, the maneuvering vent and their respective lines are checked for free and easy movement and to see that the panels themselves are secure. Then one must inspect the temperature telltales and the pyrometer coupling.

76. *What if the telltales are black?*

You'll probably have to cancel the flight, though it might depend on which temperature range had been exceeded. The telltale (or template) has four little openings, each marked by a particular temperature. If the maximum permissible temperature has been exceeded and all four openings are black, you will definitely have to cancel the flight and call for a fabric test.

77. *What is the best weather for ballooning?*

Days with light winds and clear skies are the most fun. Inflation becomes increasingly difficult with winds over five knots, though with a strong ground crew one can inflate with winds up to about fifteen knots. The problem is not so much at the liftoff stage—though a balloon can go out of control on the ground quite easily—but in coming down, since landings in a strong wind present a considerable challenge to a balloonist's skill and can be dangerous to the inexperienced.

78. *Does the gondola swing about in strong winds?*

The wind doesn't really make too much difference, since once you are off the ground, the entire rig is highly stable. The gondola of a balloon makes an excellent platform for motion pictures, far better than an airplane and smoother than a helicopter.

Fabled Le Geant,
Nadar's giant balloon,
constructed in France in 1863.

Car of Nadar's Le Geant *balloon.*

79. *Is it quiet in a balloon?*

When the burner is off in a hot-air balloon, it is very quiet, but when the burner is being used, it is quite noisy. Reckon about fifty seconds of silence and ten seconds of noise to maintain an agreeable altitude on an average day. Gas balloons are virtually silent all the time. The peace and quiet is what attracts many people to ballooning.

80. *Is ballooning quieter than soaring?*

Considerably so. Soaring is also a rather busy sport, since one has to monitor the instruments much more closely and work to maintain altitude by finding thermals and lift. One is also constantly on the lookout for a good place to land if one travels any distance from the airport.

81. *Why haven't you said much about gas balloons?*

Mostly because the expense of gas-balloon flight puts it out of the average taxpayer's price range. The military, who get their flying free, run a number of projects and sponsor others with gas balloons.

82. *How much money is involved in operating gas balloons?*

Using coal gas, which is flammable, you'd expect to pay between $300 and $400 *per flight*. Hydrogen, also highly flammable, is the best lifting gas, and costs would be slightly more than double—say $900 *per flight*. Finally there's helium, an inert gas which in terms of lift is better than coal gas but not as good as hydrogen, and costs would be around $1,200 to $1,500 *per flight*.

83. *How many people could go on such a trip?*

The figures quoted are for a typical two-place gas balloon and are all for a single trip, since once the flight is over, the gas is gone. A single flight in a helium-filled balloon could pay for your entire training for a commercial free balloon pilot license, rated hot-air.

84. *What does "experimental" mean when applied to a balloon?*

The experimental category is one provided by the FAA to permit an individual or a firm to develop a design while flying it. A balloon with an experimental designation has not yet been type-certificated by the government. Some experimental designs are light years ahead of conventional certificated designs; however, many more are probably not quite as good.

The first manned balloon ascension occurred November 21, 1783. The aerostat was built by the Montgolfier brothers and is pictured here at Château de la Muette.

85. *What do Montgolfier and Charlier indicate in relation to balloons?*

Around two hundred years ago, hot-air balloons were invented by the Montgolfier brothers, while gas balloons—using hydrogen—were invented by a physicist called Charles. The people of the time referred to hot-air balloons as *Montgolfières* and hydrogen balloons as *Charlières*, terms which traditionalists among aeronauts use to this day.

86. *Exactly when and where was the first manned balloon flight made?*

In France, in November 1783.

87. *To what modern aircraft is a balloon most comparable?*

A helicopter. Although a balloon can't actually hover—except in windless conditions—it can maintain a highly precise altitude.

88. *Can balloons land on water?*

Provided the balloon is kept inflated, water landings are possible. However, it is wise to avoid water except in an emergency.

Helicopter flight is the nearest form of aviation to aerostation. Aeronauts claim that balloons can maintain altitude more efficiently than their rotary-winged cousins.

89. *How come there's so little information about ballooning?*

Modern ballooning, that is, hot-air ballooning, is a comparatively recent phenomenon—the result, curiously enough, of a military procurement order in 1961.

90. *How exactly did the modern hot-air balloon develop?*

The navy had a requirement for a hot-air balloon as part of a series of research projects they run to keep up to date on various technologies in case they ever have need for one. Paul E. (Ed) Yost—generally recognized as the father of modern hot-air ballooning and now president of Dakota Industries in Sioux Falls, South Dakota—was then with Raven Industries, Inc., the firm that received the navy contract.

91. *Where did this contract lead?*

Yost decided to utilize modern technology, first to improve envelope fabric, and next to provide heat. The Montgolfier brothers erroneously believed that it was smoke from fire that provided lift. Consequently, they used damp stable straw, shredded wool and even old shoes to provide smoke—a factor that distressed the royal nostrils of the king and queen of France, their native land. Yost substituted a modern propane burner unit for the Montgolfier system.

92. *Has Yost designed anything else?*

Ed Yost has probably forgotten more about the design of hot-air balloons than most of us will ever know. In addition, he holds the largest number of patents connected with the business in the world. It was his reputation as a modern wizard in this area that led Malcolm Forbes to commission him to design *Forbes* magazine's record-setting balloon, the *Château de Balleroy*.

93. *You mentioned modernized envelope fabric. What was used before?*

A special weave of treated silk was used. Nylon is considerably cheaper than silk, and with modern treatment is able to disperse heat more easily without much deterioration.

94. *What is heat dispersion?*

The function of the envelope is to contain hot air. If the fabric didn't allow some of the heat to escape into the atmosphere, the envelope would deteriorate too rapidly to be useful for long.

The Château de Balleroy, France, where Malcolm Forbes' unique balloon museum is situated. Just in front of the château itself is Forbes' transAmerican hot-air balloon, which bears the same name. In foreground, being inflated, is the Heineken balloon.

95. *Could anyone build a balloon?*

Provided one were ready to spend a lot of time studying the subject, yes. But since there are a number of admirably designed balloons around, why bother? Unless, of course, you want to go into the business yourself.

96. *How many balloons are there?*

In the United States there are probably more than 700 balloons, and the number is increasing rapidly. Elsewhere, the sport is also burgeoning, especially in Europe.

97. *How do aeronauts compete?*

One of the best-known types of event is the "hare and the hounds" race, in which the lead contestant takes off, and after a short interval the remainder follow and try to land as close to the first balloon as possible.

Another popular kind of competition is a precision effort in which barographs are used. Before beginning, the organizers decide what altitudes are to be flown and for how long. The barograph records each contestant's actual flight and the balloon that comes closest wins.

A fly-off at an international balloon meet in New Mexico.

98. *Are there cross-country exercises for balloonists, as for regular pilots?*

Yes. Your thirty-minute or hour-long flight will be a "proper" cross-country, as will your solo flights. Every flight, except when you're working at a tether, is a cross-country flight. It's important to understand that aeronauts are just as much pilots as those who fly other air vehicles. While there is more to do in other types of air vehicles, the balloon pilot is in more intimate contact with the elements.

99. *Do I need to take oxygen with me on flights?*

Oxygen is not normally used below 12,000 feet. However, it should be noted that at 10,000 feet above sea level, the brain is receiving the minimum amount of oxygen required to function normally. Above this altitude, the brain gradually—and without the pilot's noticing it—loses its ability to function rationally. FAR 91.32 requires the use of supplemental oxygen if above 12,500 feet for thirty minutes or more, or if above 14,000 feet unpressurized, continuously.

While the effects of oxygen starvation vary from person to person, more than four hours at 8,000 and up to 10,000 will produce fatigue and sluggishness. Above 10,000 feet for two hours will produce poor judgment and possibly headaches.

The technical name for lack of oxygen is *hypoxia.* People who smoke cigarettes must be even more careful, since their red corpuscles—the ones that carry the oxygen—are usually saturated with carbon monoxide. Unfortunately, hemoglobin tends to combine with carbon monoxide some three hundred times more easily than it does with oxygen. Just three cigarettes can raise a normal person's apparent altitude—measured in terms of oxygen carried in the blood—from sea level to around 8,000 feet.

100. *Should smokers use oxygen at lower altitudes?*

Yes, if a pilot who smokes wants to fly high, then additional oxygen should be taken.

101. *Why do you carry wine or champagne on board?*

The reason behind the tradition is that in the early days, when balloons often landed in rural territory, the local people had never seen or heard of them. Consequently, they reacted with fear at seeing something come in upon them from the skies. (How would you feel if a flying saucer landed in your backyard?) Frequently the balloons were attacked with pitchforks,

Pioneer balloonists lost equipment to terrified peasants who reacted fearfully to the skyborne apparatus. It was discovered that champagne offered to the peasantry avoided confrontation.

This peasant custom is still followed and champagne is enjoyed at the conclusion of a flight.

which destroyed them. The early aeronauts found it advantageous to take wine to offer to the local citizens on touchdown. The custom still has merit.

Balloonists today are still very happy indeed about not knowing where they are going to land. Unless it's a record distance attempt, it's not going to be *that* far away. Unless you are attempting a transatlantic flight, you will most likely land on earth. It is also very likely you will meet up with other people—total strangers—and as you will probably want to use their telephone to call the pickup truck, you arrive with something to get the party rolling. There is a good reason for serious aeronauts dutifully carrying champagne aloft as part of the flight equipment. This traditional drink for festive occasions makes it easy for everyone to relax and enjoy some time together before getting on with their day. After all, it isn't every day of the week that strangers drop in unexpectedly by balloon. And the champagne makes everybody feel wanted—especially when it's free.

PART II:

Preparing for the Balloon Pilot's License

Flight Briefing

Systems and Procedures
for Montgolfier Aerostats

I am indebted to Bob Waligunda for letting me adapt this flight briefing
from the training program developed by Sky Promotions Balloon
Training Center, Princeton, New Jersey.

"The objective of flight training is to let
pilots safely enjoy the alien environment of
the skies."

Duncan Holmes

*T*he business of getting a balloon up into the air and then
back onto the ground is a series of distinct yet interrelated operations. In
driving a car or flying a powered aircraft, these procedures may be easily
observed. To start a car you must first open the door (perhaps unlock it),
and settle yourself into the seat. Before settling into the seat of an airplane,
you'll have made a walkaround—a visual inspection to see that all's well
before you leave the ground.

This flight briefing is designed to enable you to learn and understand
the procedures required for the safe handling of the modern hot-air balloon.
Each procedure relates directly to the safe and efficient operation of the
flight and, if used to supplement regular tuition, should allow you to complete each phase of flight training expeditiously.

There are six main steps, called flight procedures,* which deal in a
general way with everything you need to do from before your lift-off until
after you land. Checklists for these procedures are included in the appendix.
There are also ten maneuvers, the actions you'll eventually put together in
order to accomplish those procedures, whether climbing from lift-off, level-

---

* 1. Preflight   4. Lift-off
   2. Inflation   5. Landing
   3. Pre—lift-off   6. Postlanding

ing at an altitude, using blast valve or cruise valve, determining when to use the maneuvering vent, and so on.

Then there is a review of emergencies and what to check for to prevent their occurrence. And there are also some notes which deal with the systems of the aerostat: each working part, what it does and how you use it.

In order to acquire the certification issued by the FAA, both a written exam and a flight test are required, and a student pilot certificate is necessary once you get started. Balloon training is, by and large, conducted efficiently throughout the country, and unlike other areas of flight training, your balloon instructor is probably not trying to build up hours in order to get a good job with more pay somewhere else.

Because instructors in this field are usually directly involved in the art, you are more likely to enjoy extended preflight and postflight briefings in which you'll acquire the sort of firsthand information that makes the difference between an adequate pilot and a skilled one.

Flight training is best when ground and flight instruction are correlated, and this is another area in which this flight briefing should serve as a useful reference. It should, however, be understood that this flight briefing is not a particular codex to balloon flight training, even though the format has been successfully used as a basis for flight training by one of the leading balloon schools in the East.

Students should always remain aware that it is the balloon that groundlings are staring at, not the people in the gondola. And as Bob Waligunda puts it: "You really do have to make sure that your ego doesn't get as inflated as your balloon."

FLIGHT PROCEDURES

Preflight

A number of tasks must be completed before the pilot goes ahead with inflation. In hot-air balloons the first thing is the matter of fuel: Is there sufficient fuel available for the operation? Are the lines clear? Are there any leaks in the system?

If the fuel situation is deemed in order, the next question is whether the burner system—which uses the fuel to provide hot air to the envelope—is in working order. Therefore, the items to be checked include the proper working of the pilot light, the blast valve and cruise valve, and the pressure regulator if fitted.*

Like airplanes, aerostats must also contend with loading factors, which depend on the amount of lift available and the outside air temperature. Ground school instruction will have covered the properties of gases and the effects of the atmosphere on their function. Now comes the practical side: What is the gross weight, and what is the altitude limitation for this balloon here and now?

Fortunately for those whose mathematical ability is somewhat limited, most manufacturers provide charts giving the maximum authorized operating limits for sustained operation. A typical chart will give gross load in pounds together with the ambient temperature listed in tens of degrees Fahrenheit. An example is shown.

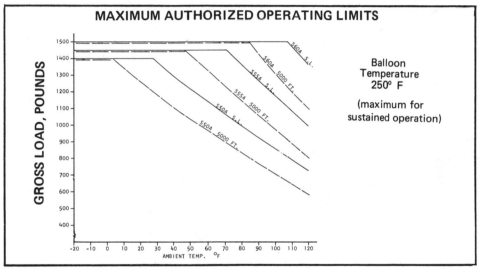

Operating temperature chart showing maximum authorized operating limit for Raven series aerostats. Note maximum temperature of 250° F, for sustained operations.

These questions dealt with, next comes the visual inspection of the fabric, the ground handling lines (each should be clear and untangled) and the crown line (red) and the checks required inside the envelope itself. The deflation port should be closed. The maneuvering vent should be sealed. Temperature telltales (if fitted; some balloon makers are too cheap and rely on the pilot's eagle eyes and a temperature gauge instead) checked okay.

---

* When modern hot-air balloons were originally introduced, no pressure regulator was provided. Later models were fitted with regulators, but the practice has been discontinued in new balloons.

The balloon envelope is unstowed from its bag in the gondola . . .

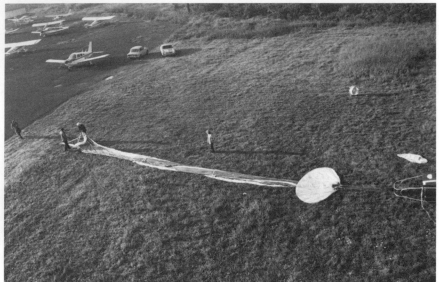

. . . and carefully unfolded . . .

. . . to its full length.

Then it is spread out . . .

. . . and visual inspection of lines and fabric made.

Clearing gas lines is a colorful and necessary procedure, as liquid gas evaporates in the cool air.

Finally there is the gondola and its instrumentation. Are the instruments secured? And have the a) altimeter, b) variometer, c) pyrometer and d) compass been checked and/or set?

In the gondola: Is the drag line aboard and secured? Are igniters (two minimum) all working and aboard?

And finally, after the last of these checks is made, the cold inflation fan should be ready and fueled for operation.

Inflation

As pilot in command (even during training), you are responsible for all activity at the launch site. You'll eventually have to do this after you've got your license, so you'd better get used to it now. This includes supervision and briefing of your ground crew—even if, at the beginning, they know more about what's happening than you do.

For ease of inflation be sure to position the gondola in such a way that the balloon envelope can be spread out downwind. This is particularly important if there is any wind.

Having checked fuel flow, visual inspection should be thorough, since apart from the inefficient use of heat, any questionable integrity of the fabric is a cause for concern. A hot-air balloon will fly even if punctured with holes, but it's not going to do a very good job of it, and could bring you to grief.

Now you're ready for inflation—cold inflation.

While there are still a number of traditionalists who eschew the use of fans for cold inflation, preferring the time-honored method of "flopping" cold air into the envelope, the use of a fan is more sensible. True, fans are noisy, smelly, and some are downright dangerous—given the chance some will even eat up your fingers and chew handling lines or children with abandon. But they are virtually the only way in which to get a good bubble of cold air inside the envelope into which the hot air can be injected. Ideally, before hot inflation occurs, the envelope should be at least three-quarters full of cold air, and on windy days it should be completely full.

It's difficult not to sympathize with the traditionalists on the matter of fans, and in the case of two-cycle fans they have a point. The two-cycle engine which propels the prop also exhausts a fine mist of oil—mixed with its fuel for proper lubrication—which may cause damage to the fabric after repeated usage. So if you have settled on a fan, make sure you get a four-cycle powered engine. Also check to see that the fan itself is well guarded, since a good fan moves a considerable volume of air and can pick up scattered stones, lines, and loose apparel as it does its work. It is

Cold-air inflation is the first step, modern aeronauts favoring a motor-driven fan to the traditional method of "flopping."

Fan blows bubble of cold air into the envelope . . .

. . . allowing visual inspection inside of lines, Velcro seals and temperature telltales.

In foreground is maneuvering vent, which will be closed off prior to hot-air inflation. Gondola and fan can be seen outside the seemingly modernistic cathedral curves of partially inflated aerostat.

Pilot is extremely careful to direct blast of hot air into center of cold air and away from fabric once hot-air inflation begins.

especially important to warn children of the risks involved in all stages of inflation. Also see to it that dog owners keep their animals properly leashed.

The object of the cold-air inflation is to fill the balloon with cold air so as not to burn the fabric during the hot inflation stage, as well as to extend your visual inspection and to check that the basic systems are in order. This means that in addition to further checks of the fabric, you also make sure that the deflation port strap is clear, the maneuvering vent line is clear, and that both the deflation port and the maneuvering vent are sealed. (You should double-check these last two to make sure the seal is holding up under inflation.) In some balloons sealing is automatic—that is, both deflation port and maneuvering vent tend to stay sealed under inflation. Nevertheless, be sure to make this check.

It is worth noting at this point that all crew involved with inflation should be provided with gloves or gauntlets, and the person in charge of hot-air inflation in addition should be provided with sunglasses or goggles for eye protection, and a long-sleeved shirt. Furthermore, the ground crew should understand that ground handling lines must never be wrapped around the hand—one or more knots in the line will provide handholds which can be released easily. Lastly, some sort of skull protection should be provided for the flying crew—the pilot in command must have a helmet, and it is a good idea to provide helmets for other flight members if a high-wind landing is expected.

Once you are satisfied that all is well within the fabric cathedral, you are ready to start the hot-air inflation. Keep the cold-air fan on, since this will help spread out the hot air rather than let it bubble. (When this happens and nothing is done, damage to the fabric can occur at the "hot spot" and the balloon can set itself up for oscillation as it erects; and an oscillating balloon is more difficult to tame than a bull in a china shop!)

For a high-wind inflation be sure that the gondola is secured or anchored until you are ready to go. Chasing a partially inflated balloon in a wind is no fun. Also see the note about false lift (page 51). Finally, make sure if for any reason you have to abort the inflation, that the landing area—which is what your lift-off area will become—is clear of spectators who could get hurt by the fabric whipping in the wind.

Keep the burner going in blasts until the balloon is in an upright position.

Aborting:

If for any reason you need to abort the inflation, a) open the deflation port with the rip strap (red), and b) ensure that crew positions are maintained until envelope completely deflates. For reinflation, go back to the beginning by first positioning the gondola and paying attention to proper fuel feed.

Pre–Lift-off

The balloon is now upright, and there are just a few more checks to be made before you lift off. These checks concern many items you have been dealing with before, but this is your last chance to see to them before leaving the ground.

First, continue your interest in the lines connecting the maneuvering vent and deflation port to the gondola so that they are not caught or tangled with each other. They should have been secured so that they are not inadvertently opened. Similarly, you will maintain further visual inspection of fabric integrity and also check that both the maneuvering vent and deflation port are properly sealed while hot-air inflation proceeds.

Now it's back to the fuel system. Draw fuel from each source and select the fullest tank for lift-off. If you have a double burner system (fuel tank to burner) check that both are working properly and note the balance in the fuel reserve. Check also that tank valves are either fully on or fully off, and adjust pilot light and cruise valve as, or if, needed.

The final instrument check includes setting your altimeter. This may be set to "field zero," or what is termed QFE in the "Q" code. This is airfield pressure, and you set the altimeter to zero. If you're taking off from an airfield at which weather information is available, or where there is a control tower, you can get the exact barometric pressure at the field. This will usually give you your approximate elevation. Some pilots prefer to set the altimeter to field elevation. But whichever you do, decide on a particular method and remember what setting you have used. Your instructor will no doubt have his own preference, so consider that as well.

At this point you'll turn on the variometer—the sensitive rate-of-climb indicator which has to be set at zero.

Finally, there's the pyrometer, which, as you'll remember, is a simple thermocouple that tells you the temperature at the balloon's apex where the hottest air is. Sixty percent of the aerostat's lifting power derives from the heated air at its equator and up, and a careful eye on the pyrometer will ensure that the temperature is within limits. Too high a temperature will damage the balloon fabric and reduce its life, and with new burner systems—which pour out hot air in vast quantities—short bursts on the blast valve are the order of the day.

As mentioned earlier, some manufacturers don't supply temperature telltales. Some don't provide pyrometers either, although they should be required to, since the heat/fabric equation is of considerable interest to the aeronaut. This cheese-paring attitude is comparable to General Motors' "advertised price" of an automobile, and will only be changed by educating those who prize money above human life.

If there's a pressure regulator fitted in your fuel system, this should be set at the appropriate outflow pressure. Let your instructor demonstrate this, since pressures vary from system to system.

One last ground check is required to ensure that both ground handling lines and tether ropes are free. This is more important than its seems, since you wouldn't want to be like other unfortunate aeronauts who have snared a person at lift-off and carried them screaming skyward beneath the gondola.

Now you're almost ready.

Make sure that at least two functioning igniters are aboard (also for safety sake have some matches and/or a cigarette lighter on hand).

Lift-off

Standard:

1. Obtain equilibrium, make a note of pyrometer reading, if fitted, and of Outside Air Temperature (if OAT is supplied).

2. Check that ground crew are at station and that spectators are clear. Flight crew, if any, should be aboard and ready for lift-off.

3. Get inboard gondola and when you are ready to go, call "Clear!" much as a power pilot "clears" his prop before he starts the engine(s).

4. Using blast valve frequently and intermittently to lift off, proceed with enough heat to provide a sufficient rate of climb to clear all obstacles. *Note:* The initial rate of heating should be sufficient to insure a safe lift-off where wind shift, false lift* or increased wind velocity seem likely.

Prior to lift-off make sure nobody gets tangled with lines or gondola. Pilot in sketch will close maneuvering vent prior to making solo ascension.

---

* This condition occurs when cold air creates an airfoil shape from the envelope, gently caving in one side of the balloon by driving hot air out. *Your instructor should demonstrate this for you.*

Positive Buoyancy:

This procedure is used to overcome obstacles nearby, high winds or potential or incipient false lift.

1. Before obtaining equilibrium, brief ground crew members to hold the balloon down while additional heat is applied. *Note:* Normally 20–25°F will be sufficient, though this will depend on load.

2. At the call "Clear" ground crew will simultaneously release the balloon. (Make sure you're inboard.)

3. Monitor pyrometer and variometer immediately after lift-off is made.

Landing

Sooner or later all flights must end. To ensure that yours ends on a happy note, there is a certain amount of work to be done ahead of time. Gear must be stowed or readied. The burner requires adjustment. The fuel supply should be sufficient to complete the approach and abort the landing if necessary. Finally, you need to have selected a suitable landing site.

Like the glider pilot, the aeronaut is used to off-airport landings. If you should inadvertently land at an airport, you'd better have a radio along to advise the other fliers or the control tower of your intentions. Power pilots are not used to landing off airports these days, and most airplanes today lack the undercarriage needed to put them down safely on virgin soil.

Procedure for the Approach:

1. All loose gear should be stowed. Drag lines—*not* recommended for hot-air balloons—should be rolled up like a ball in order to fall freely, and readied for easy deployment.

2. Check fuel supply and see that all tanks are fully on.

3. Flame source should be turned up as desired. New pilot lights are adjustable. With older equipment, the cruise valve may be adjusted to provide alternate pilot light function.

4. Rely on visual references during the approach and control heat with blast valve only.

Standard Approach to Landing:

1. Set up a suitable rate of descent which will safely clear you of all obstacles and provide line-of-sight motion toward the landing area.

2. By visual reference and the controls maintain a relative position toward the landing area throughout the approach.

3. *Rate of descent should not exceed that of balloon's altitude AGL.* (For example, if AGL altitude equals 200 feet, *maximum* rate of descent should be 200 fpm.)

4. Unless there is a high wind or a small field landing, use of the maneu- vering vent should not be necessary. Its use is not, however, excluded. *Note:* The maneuvering vent is really only to be used when it is absolutely re- quired. A hot-air balloon can be con- trolled within fine limits by judicious use of the blast valve.

Steep Approach to Landing:

This procedure is used in order to clear high obstacles, power or tele- phone lines, land in small areas.

1. Establish level flight at the lowest safe altitude possible as your intended landing area draws close.

2. Immediately after the final ob- stacle is cleared, fully open maneuver- ing vent for an interval sufficient to initiate the descent; that will permit time for aborting the landing with reheating.

3. Reheat envelope promptly to con- trol touchdown rate of descent. *Note:* It is possible to make featherlight touchdowns in almost all conditions with practice.

Aborting the Approach or Descent:

Sometimes what appears to be the perfect landing spot turns out to be—on closer inspection—one that you'd rather pass up. It may be that the ground is covered with poison ivy or stinging nettles, or there may be other problems. Whatever the reason, you must make up your mind promptly, since there is no place for hovering at this crucial point in flight.

1. Use blast valve only.

2. Apply maximum heat with blast valve until descent is not merely checked, but a climb has begun.

3. Monitor pyrometer and recover in level flight at desired altitude.

Of all the maneuvers, landing an aerostat is the one which must be mastered before the fledgling pilot is truly ready. Unless a landing is properly performed, there's a risk of damaging the envelope. And what's worse, even the crew can get bruised during a clumsy landing.

A good landing takes place after a good approach has been made. Once the prelanding checks have been completed, the flight crew position them- selves, knees bent, one handhold upwind and one downwind, facing in the direction of travel.

The moments just prior to touchdown are busy ones for the pilot. The burners are off and grip is released on the burner controls. Prior to landing,

Maneuver 3:

Transition: climb to level flight (blast valve). Starting from 500-feet-per-minute rate of ascent.

1. Reduce heat supply to reduce rate of ascent at a point 500 feet below the desired altitude.

2. Progressively reduce rate of ascent one fpm per each foot of altitude gained.

3. Stabilize balloon in level flight at desired altitude.

Maneuver 4:

Transition: climb to level flight (cruise valve). Starting from a 500 fpm rate of ascent.

1. Diminish heat supply to reduce rate of ascent at a point 750 feet below desired altitude.

2. Progressively reduce rate of ascent 1.5 fpm per each foot of altitude gained.

3. Stabilize balloon in level flight at desired altitude.

Maneuver 5:

Maintaining level flight (blast or cruise valve). Check the pyrometer reading and note the variometer. A standard temperature will give you a standard altitude at which you can fly.

1. Apply sufficient heat to maintain desired altitude (or temperature).

2. To correct instability, use methods described in preceding maneuvers (1, 2, 3 and 4).

Maneuver 6:

Descent (blast valve). This maneuver should take place at not less than 500 feet AGL.

1. Reduce heat to establish a rate of descent.

2. Progressively increase rate of descent one fpm for each foot descended.

3. At 500 feet below initial altitude, a rate of descent of 500 fpm should have been achieved as you pass thru the altitude.

4. Maintain this 500 fpm rate of descent.

Maneuver 7:

Descent (cruise valve). This maneuver should take place at not less than 1,000 feet AGL.

1. Reduce heat to establish rate of descent.

2. Progressively increase rate of descent one fpm for each 1.5 feet descended.

3. At 750 feet below initial altitude, a rate of descent of 500 fpm will be established.

4. Maintain this rate of 500 fpm.

Maneuver 8:

Transition: from descent to level flight (blast valve). Start from a 500 fpm rate of descent.

1. Apply heat to initiate a slower rate of descent at a point 500 feet above desired altitude.

2. Progressively reduce rate of descent one fpm for each foot descended.

3. Stabilize balloon in level flight at desired altitude.

Maneuver 9:

Transition: descent to level flight (cruise valve). Start from a 500 fpm rate of descent.

1. Apply heat to initiate a slower rate of descent at a point 750 feet above desired altitude.

2. Progressively reduce rate of descent one fpm for each 1.5 feet descended.

3. Stabilize balloon in level flight at desired altitude.

Maneuver 10:

Terminal velocity descent. This maneuver is designed to make you familiar with the terminal velocity rate of descent of your balloon and should not be undertaken at less than 5,000 feet AGL. The pilot light or cruise valve can be turned up to provide a flame source during descent and the blast valve can be used intermittently to prevent freeze up during the maneuver.

1. Allow envelope to cool and the balloon to descend to the terminal rate.

2. Monitor throat area to observe possible caving in, so that when you ignite burner(s) you don't burn or melt the fabric on reheating.

3. Adjust pressure regulator, if fitted, to 100 percent.

4. At a minimum of 2,000 feet AGL, use blast valve steadily until the rate of descent is reduced to 300 fpm. Thereafter continue with blast valve as needed to level off with a minimum loss of altitude.

Actual velocity in this maneuver is in the range of descent rate of a sport parachute.

FLIGHT SYSTEMS

Burner System

Pilot Light:

The pilot light should be fully on at all times and can be adjusted. It can be reignited by a striker or a secondary heat device (such as matches). Adjust flame as necessary.

Cruise Valve:

Before using, turn cruise valve completely off. Crack valve very slightly and open. Pilot light should ignite gas. Adjust to produce between six and ten inches of flame.

The cruise valve is used to provide a standard amount of heat to maintain a standard altitude—rather like an autopilot controlling heat.

If the pilot light goes out and cannot be reignited, you can slowly turn up the cruise valve and light the main jets of the burner assembly. Once the main jets are lit, this should relight the pilot. If it still won't reignite, fly with a low cruise valve setting.

Note: a) Regulate the cruise valve to produce continuous heat and monitor the pyrometer. b) When changing altitude, and at frequent intervals at other times, readjustment may be necessary. Constant monitoring of the valve and pyrometer is necessary to optimize performance.

Above left: Heart of the modern burner system, the nozzles pour vast quantities of hot air on demand.

Above: Controls of the burner system are simple, the knob with the line attached being the blast valve—pull to work, with cruise valve adjacent the other side of pressure gauge.

Left: Instant hot air is provided with single burners capable of outputs up to 12,000,000 BTUs.

Blast Valve:

Before using the blast valve, always check that a fire source—i.e. pilot light, or cruise valve—is available. You don't want to be deluged with unlighted gas. Also, check to see that all balloon material is clear of the flame area.

The blast valve provides instant, intense heat on demand. Never partially open the blast valve during flight. The blast valve should be fully on, or fully off, except during inflation.

Takeoff: Except when taking off with positive buoyancy, when a short interval prior to lift-off is made to check that everything is clear, there should be a short pause within the first few feet of ascent so that any warnings of incipient foul-ups—i.e. snagged ground lines, some person caught or still holding the basket—can be remedied. Provided the ground crew is briefed, and visitors are also told what to expect, such occurrences will be unlikely.

In-flight: To maintain a desired envelope temperature, check the pyrometer and variometer, and vary the length of the blast and/or the interval of time in between blasts. This technique is quickly learned with practice and it will be found that altitude can be maintained to the nearest foot more easily than in a helicopter.

Ice: Frequent use of the blast valve is the best method to avoid the possibility of freezing. Keep a close visual check to see whether icing is taking place, since the cooling of the valve caused by restricted flow will cause frequent readjustment. If not corrected, a freeze-up can occur.

Landing: The more accurate altitude control required, especially near the ground, is achieved by using short, frequent blasts.

Instruments

Pyrometer:

Use to monitor heat at the top of the balloon.

1. Always note reading at initial equilibrium prior to takeoff so that *a*) a safe climb can be made without overheating, and *b*) you will have a temperature reference during flight. *This is vital when flying in warm weather.*

2. Use temperature cooling to forecast changes in altitude.

3. As a cross reference, the pyrometer may be used to determine whether changes in altitude are due to heat input or to atmospheric action.

4. The pyrometer is a secondary instrument reference.

Variometer:

No accurate reference can be established with the variometer in flight if it has not been activated and set at zero prior to takeoff.

1. The variometer is the primary instrument reference.

2. Its sensitivity varies and adjustments in reference are needed for efficient use.

Basic instrument panel is—from left to right—electric variometer, which notes instantly up/down movement, pyrometer—a thermocouple provides temperature reading at balloon's apex. At right is altimeter, which records operating altitude. Gas tanks are stowed here beneath panel.

Another method of dealing with instrumentation. Here instrument module is fitted close to burner controls.

Altimeter:

An altimeter is a sensitive aneroid barometer and should be set prior to lift-off (see Maneuver 3).

1. While an altimeter will give exact and immediate *trend* information (i.e. up or down), lag as to rate (i.e. how much) is normal.

2. This instrument lets you know your distance above the ground and is a secondary instrument reference.

Maneuvering Vent

The maneuvering vent is an opening in the side of the balloon which is used to release hot air and thus reduce the total lift. Some new balloons have adopted a Vent/Top in which the vent and deflation port functions are combined. These are good to use in calm weather.

The maneuvering vent is designed to self-seal; however, in certain balloons it will not fully close after initial use, and a small amount of hot air may continue to escape, increasing fuel consumption.

Uses: The vent may be used to initiate a steady state of altitude from a climb. This is not the most economical way to deal with the problem, since greater sensitivity in heating would permit the balloon to reach the same altitude. It is used this way in competitions, however.

Maneuvering vent is used to reduce lifting capacity of balloon by venting hot air. It is designed to self-seal after use. Some modern balloons use a self-sealing Vent/Top, in which deflation port serves both purposes.

The vent is used to initiate a letdown once an appropriate landing place has been selected. Desired loss of lift is provided by varying the amount the vent is opened and/or the length of time it remains open.

To begin with, try to use the same amount of opening, and vary the time held open. When releasing the vent line, make a visual check to ensure the vent has returned to the closed position. Do not worry if the balloon starts to rotate about the vertical axis, as this happens occasionally.

Landing: The use of the vent provides a more rapid descent than normal cooling, though there is a slight lag in its effect. In landing, or when using the vent near the ground, this rate of descent must be compensated for by the application of heat (use blast valve) before a too-excessive rate of descent builds up. *Rate of descent should be reduced by one foot per minute for each foot descended,* as a general rule. For example, if you are descending at 200 fpm at 200 feet AGL, you should be down to 100 fpm by the time you reach 100 feet AGL. Your instructor will go into this in greater detail.

Deflation Port (Rip Panel)

The deflation port is used to empty the balloon of hot air on landing so that the occupants won't be dragged across the ground in a breeze, and to prevent the balloon from taking off again once it has landed. It may be likened to the "lift-dump" mechanisms used by jet aircraft on touchdown, to ensure they are finished flying.

Note: Since the deflation port permits for the massive evacuation of hot air from the balloon, it is obvious that extreme care must be taken to prevent any prior opening of this port before it is needed.

The deflation port must be checked to see it is secure at each stage of preinflation, partial inflation, and pretakeoff. If Velcro fasteners are used their condition should be checked prior to each inflation and after each flight.

In a normal landing, the rip line for opening should be used to deflate on contact with the ground. This should be done rapidly—and sufficiently— to prevent ground travel.

In a high-wind landing, *provided the rate of descent is minimal,* deflation may take place several feet above the ground, depending on the size of the landing area, wind speed and local terrain.

Once used, no further attempt should be made to reheat the envelope.

Deflation port Velcro seal is carefully checked prior to each flight, as performance eventually breaks down. Replacement schedule is strictly adhered to.

Center is deflation port, which is ripped open . . .

. . . on landing to permit hot air to vent free.

Managing Fuel

It may have something to do with the mating activities of a techno-logical species, but fuel mismanagement has been the apparent cause of cars running out of gas and aircraft running out of sky since they were invented. Unless stranded in a desert or in a blizzard, the effects of such carelessness are not of too much consequence in an automobile. In an airplane the results can be hazardous: the same goes for a balloon.

There is absolutely no need to run out of fuel during a flight, and in addition to the various instruments that provide information, the best gauge of all is worn on one's wrist. The ordinary wristwatch is highly adequate to inform you of your fuel consumption provided a) that you make a note of the time you started inflation and lifted off, and b) that you know what the average amount of flying time is expected to be in your equipment considering the number of tanks you have aboard.

The following procedures have been designed to make sure that you, at least, will not run out of fuel while airborne.

Fuel management is a matter of common sense and the best fuel gauge is the watch on your wrist. Fuel tanks are specially constructed to carry high-pressure gas.

1. Except under special circum-stances, all fuel tanks on board will be filled to capacity.

2. All tanks on board will be con-nected to the burner system, whereby no connecting or disconnecting of tanks takes place while airborne.*

3. As part of the pre–lift-off checks, fuel will be drawn and checked from each tank to insure availability from each source. The fullest tank will be selected for takeoff.

4. In flight, each tank will be used successively until all are depleted to approximately 30 percent capacity. At this time all tanks will be turned on. If any tank is deliberately used until empty, it should be kept closed once it's disconnected to prevent moisture contamination.

5. Tank valves should always be turned fully on or fully off. This avoids the risk of a freeze-up.

---

* Obviously, if you've got extra fuel on board for a long flight, you'll disconnect and reconnect as necessary. Don't forget the wrenches when you take off.

Visual References

1. Visual references are the absolute primary reference, and instrument references are used to build proficient visual flight reference. With the exception of altitude flying, most ballooning is done by the seat of your pants.

2. In order to maximize your effectiveness, face in the direction you're moving. This way you'll see power or telephone lines before you run into them.

3. In order to make sure you don't run into the side of hills, check altitude variation by sighting a point approximately 20 degrees below the horizon. This should be done at right angles to the direction you're traveling in as well, so that drift motion will not confuse you.

4. During your descent for landing, pick a point on the ground that is neither moving nor below your line of sight. You can then determine your projected point of touchdown.

Visual references and the ability to understand what the eye sees are vital techniques for good landings. Not too high . . .

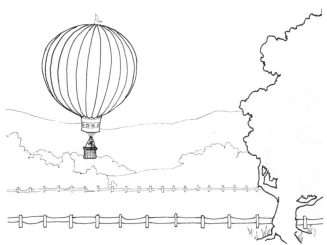

. . . not too low . . .

. . . but just right. A good landing starts with a good approach.

Emergencies

Burner and fuel system procedures

Check the following in the event of a malfunction:

1. Pilot light—adjustment and fuel
flow
2. Cruise valve
3. Blast valve
4. Tank valve   *Controls*
5. Valve icing   **1.** Maneuvering vent
6. Fuel leakage   **2.** Deflation port

Instruments   *Other*
1. Pyrometer   **1.** Excessive heat
2. Altimeter   **2.** Landings with high rate of
3. Variometer   descent
4. Compass (if required)   **3.** High-wind landings

Concluding Observations

Ballooning is not a science, it's an art, and balloon flying is an anticipatory sort of process in which your ability to sense the atmosphere counts more than your ability to push buttons or pull switches on time.

As a general rule, don't bother to inflate unless you're happy to land in the wind that is there. When marginal conditions exist, or there is any doubt in your mind about whether to fly, *don't go*. The greatest danger occurs in flying when there is pressure on you to go, even though the weather may not be quite right.

It is for this reason that balloonists always qualify whether they will fly at a particular time on a particular day with these words: *Wind and weather permitting.*

Rules and Regulations
or, Doing It By the Book

*M*aking rules for other people to live by seems to provide job opportunities for those who put themselves in charge. Regrettably, this also includes ballooning.

The FARs (as the Federal Aviation Regulations are known) are the rules under which everyone has to fly within the United States. Like the Bible, the FARs are worth a complete reading, if only to make you aware of how complicated we have managed to make flying.

This information is packaged by the Federal Aviation Administration (FAA), and while the entire FARs don't have to be committed to memory, you do need to have knowledge of the parts that apply to balloonists. These are as follows:

PART 1:   basic terminology
PART 31:   airworthiness standards relating to manned free balloons
PART 61:   numerous rules about flying
PART 71:   Federal Airways, Controlled Airspace and Reporting Points
PART 91:   General Operating and Flight Rules
PART 101:   moored balloons, kites, unmanned rockets and unmanned free balloons
PART 430:   accidents and accident reporting

Part 1 deals with definitions of the language used in the FARs. If you're not familiar with a particular term, chances are it'll be listed here. There's also an extensive listing of abbreviations and symbols. Interestingly, Part 1 also contains the rules of construction for air vehicles. Part 1 should be read carefully, as should Part 31, which deals with airworthiness standards for manned free balloons.

Part 61 deals with pilot certificates. It covers every type of certificate and the skills required to obtain each one. Pilot privileges and limitations are also listed, and you should be familiar with them. For example, as a private pilot with a free balloon rating, you are only permitted to fly a helicopter as a student (and you'll need a Third-Class Medical), unless you have obtained the appropriate certification previously. Balloon pilots and glider pilots have no need for a medical examination. To fly as a student when you are already a balloon pilot, in any air vehicle other than a glider, will mean taking a Third-Class Medical examination. If you're warm, if you can walk, and you are not psychotic, alcoholic, epileptic, heart diseased, etc., you can usually pass that Third-Class Medical. You must also not be blind.

Part 61 provides the details of medical examinations. Part 67 outlines the actual medical standards required, and the keeping of logbooks. The logbook provides details of each flight—for example, whether you were under instruction. Logged flight instruction means that the instructor has checked what you've written in your logbook and has applied his signature with his license number to authorize the entry as factually correct. Just about everything to do with flying is spelled out in this section.

In 1974 the FARs were revised, and some balloon pilots with certificates issued before that date may find themselves out in the cold. Part 61.7 specifically deals with obsolete certificates and ratings and 61.9 et seq. go into the matter of exchanges and reissuance.

Part 71 deals with designation of Federal Airways, Controlled Airspace and Reporting Points, and is largely a handbook for those who are interested in bureaucratic rules.

Part 91 contains the rules for flight within the United States—General Operating and Flight Rules, as the book says. It also contains the single most important rule in the book. This is 91.3, which states very specifically that *the pilot in command of an aircraft is directly responsible for, and is the final authority as to, the operation of that aircraft.* It also states that the pilot in command may *deviate from any rule of this subpart or of Subpart B to the extent required to meet* [an] *emergency.*

In other words, *you* as the pilot are responsible and *you* have the final say in flying. The rulemakers admit that the final word should be with the person in charge of the air machine, not the person in charge of machinery on the ground. If you should need to break the rules in order to maintain the *safe* operation of your balloon, that's the rule that gives you permission to do it. However, you had better be ready to provide chapter and verse as to why it was necessary.* Pilots who can't, tend to get the entire rule book thrown at them, and that can ruin their flying for a while.

---

* The guys who write the rules are great Monday morning quarterback artists.

Flight rules are also covered in this section, with details concerning both visual and instrument flight rules. You should know what the law allows. You are not supposed to go instrument flying with a balloon, since it confuses Air Traffic Control.

If you should need to go IFR (Instrument Flight Rules) for an instrument ascension through clouds on a record attempt, Center (the local air traffic control center) will usually permit it, provided they've had advance notice of your need. Talk to them before you go up though, since controlled airspace begins at 14,500 feet, and in some areas at 12,000 feet.

Part 91 also covers the requirements for proper balloon maintenance, how it is supposed to be carried out and by whom, as well as information on the operation of large, turbine-powered multi-engine aircraft.

Part 93 (not listed above) is for further reading and gives details of special air traffic rules. The specifics of special VFR (Visual Flight Rule) minimums listed in 93.111 and 93.113 are worth a glance. Subpart K of 93—High Density Traffic Airports—details special procedures to be followed at busy airports, but you shouldn't be there, anyway.

Part 101 is another section worthy of your attention. It deals with tethered, captive, or—as the book says—moored balloons, kites, unmanned rockets, and unmanned free balloons.

Finally, there is Part 430. This deals with the reporting of accidents and what constitutes one. Many criteria which you might suppose would constitute an accident often do not. The essential data are in Part 430.2, which deals with definitions. You should be familiar with the whole section.

If you want to buy certain parts of the FARs, you can, as the FAA has elected to convert the FARs from a volume to an individual parts system. Volume I now becomes Part 1 and is available for $3.00 (plus 75¢ for mailing outside the United States). From Volume IV comes Part 31, but you have to purchase the entire volume, which is $5.00 (enclose $1.25 extra postage outside the United States). Similarly you need to purchase Volume IX for Part 61, and Volume XI for Part 71, which deals with the designation of Federal Airways, Controlled Airspace and Reporting Points. Parts 91 and 101 can both be found in Volume VI, though they may be purchased separately. Orders for the above should be directed to Superintendent of Documents, U.S. Government Printing Office, Washington, D.C. 20409.

Another important book to read through is the AIM—*Airman's Information Manual*. This is an operational flight manual and contains everything you ever wanted to know about flying within our National Airspace System.

It comes in four parts and is periodically updated. The FAA expects you to have a pretty good knowledge of what it contains, even if most of it may not apply to you. You're supposed to know what it's for and where you can look things up.

Part 1 of the AIM deals with air traffic control, how flights are operated, and procedures affecting pilots, including the fundamentals of basic flight operation. There's also educational and training material, and the book is called *Basic Flight Manual: ATC Quarterly Procedures*. (It is updated, as its title suggests, four times a year.)

Part 2 is about places you can land. Issued twice a year, it covers all airfields, heliports and seaplane bases in the United States, Puerto Rico and the Virgin Islands. Part 2 is also useful for its information on telephone sources for current weather conditions. It contains a listing of commercial radio stations of one hundred watts or more that can be used for direction-finding purposes.

Parts 3 and 3A contain operational data and NOTAMS—Notices to Airmen—considered essential to flight safety. It lists radio navigational aids and their frequencies and includes specific procedures for instrument pilots. Also included are substitute route structure details, sectional chart bulletins and special general and area notices. None of this is of much interest to aeronauts, but you're expected to know about it. Finally, there are details of any new or permanently closed airports, plus suggested Area Navigation Routes. Part 3 is issued every four weeks, Part 3A every two weeks. Part 3A also contains supplemental information to Parts 3 and 4.

Part 4 of the AIM is issued twice a year and includes many things that were left out of the other sections. It has graphic notices and supplemental data, as well as a useful list of abbreviations—important for reading this type of literature. It also includes special notices such as the locations of parachute-jump areas and the times they may be used. VOR (Very high frequency Omni-directional Range) receiver checkpoints—both ground and airborne—are also found here.

Get your instructor to show you the AIM. Probably your flight-training school will have one. Certainly every FSS (Flight Service Station) is supposed to have an up-to-date copy of the AIM, and as pilot in command, you are expected to check out the NOTAMS each time you fly.*

---

* Jeppesen & Co. at 8025 40th Avenue, Denver, Colorado 80207, who provide charts and maps for aviators, haven't gotten around to producing a special package for balloon pilots, but no doubt they soon will. You should then become a Jeppesen subscriber like almost every other aviator around. (In the meantime, you can, of course, subscribe to "J-Aid" service—issued by Jeppesen & Co.)

Professionals are those who perform an activity—whatever it happens to be—for a livelihood. They are expected to be good. The main point about professionalism is to ensure that everyone knows what's going on and that no one gets hurt in the activity.

The written examination required is part of this "professional" system. In answering the questions, however, you'll come across some obviously outrageous suggested answers. Out of four multiple choice questions, you will probably find that questions two and four are related by some logic. Then you'll discover that questions one and four basically contradict one another in their assumptions.

The most accurate way to get to the correct answer is first to distinguish which answer (or answers) can immediately be eliminated. On a rare occasion they'll try to trap you with muddled semantics. The best way to find the right answers is to look more deeply into the logic of the question—and, of course, to know the rules.

The FAA demands a minimum grade of 70 percent on the exam, so try to figure out what they are saying in each paragraph. It's often confusing, but it will give you a thrill when you pass with a 90 percent, which you can do if you put a little time aside for thinking the questions through.

Federal Aviation Regulations and Obtaining a License

*T*he following is a brief outline of what the Federal Aviation Regulations require of all pilots. Before you even start your flight training, you need a student pilot's certificate. You may not act as pilot in command, or as a required pilot flight-crew member in a flying machine of United States registry, unless you possess a current pilot certificate issued to you under Part 61 of the FARs (see preceding chapter).

To graduate to *private pilot* with a free balloon rating, you will require at least ten hours of flight time plus ground-school training. Additional training and flight time will enable you to get your *commercial pilot* certificate with a free balloon rating, and this allows you to teach and fly for money.

Student Pilot Certificate

Subpart C—61.81 et seq.

1. You have to be at least fourteen years old to get a student pilot certificate limited to the operation of a free balloon or glider.

2. You have to be able to read, speak and understand English.

3. You have to certify that you have no known medical defect that might make you unable to pilot a free balloon or glider. (You can take a Third-Class Medical if you want to, but it's not mandatory.)

4. Student pilot certificates are issued by FAA inspectors and by designated pilot examiners.

5. Requirements for solo flight are spelled out in regulation 61.87 of the FARs, and before you solo you will have to complete the requirements of this section. To fly solo means flight time in which either you are the sole occupant of the aircraft, or in which you act as pilot in command of an air vehicle requiring more than one flight crew member.

Before you solo you will have to show your instructor that you are familiar with the flight rules of Part 91 of the FARs—General Operating and Flight Rules—which apply to student solo flight. You must also have received ground and flight instruction in the following:

a) flight preparation, including preflighting the balloon

b) operation of hot air or gas source, use of ballast, valves, maneuvering vent and rip panels, as appropriate

c) lift-offs and ascents, descents and landings, emergency use of rip panel—which may be simulated.

Instruction must be given by an authorized flight instructor or holder of a commercial pilot certificate with a lighter-than-air category and free balloon class rating.

6. Student pilots may only fly a balloon under the supervision of a qualified instructor. Student pilots are not permitted to carry passengers or to fly for hire.

Private Pilot Certificate

Subpart D—61.101 et seq.

1. To get a free balloon private pilot's certificate, you must be at least sixteen years old.

2. You must be able to read, speak and understand English.

3. You must certify that you have no known medical defect that might make you unable to fly a free balloon. (You may take a Third-Class Medical, but it's not mandatory.)

4. You must pass a written test as required by regulation 61.105. This covers:

a) FARs applicable to private free balloon pilot privileges, limitations and flight operations

b) use of aeronautical charts and the magnetic compass for free balloon navigation

c) recognition of various weather conditions; how to obtain and use aviation weather briefings appropriate to free balloon operations

d) operating principles and procedures of free balloons, including gas and hot-air inflation systems.

5. You must have logged instruction from an authorized flight instructor in the following procedures, and your logbook must be signed by an authorized flight instructor who has found you competent to perform each maneuver safely as a private pilot:

a) rigging and mooring, including ground handling, preflight checks, cold- and hot-air inflation

b) operation of the burner system, if airborne heater is carried

c) ascents and descents

d) landings and emergencies, including use of the ripcord, which may be simulated.

6. Regulation 61.117 details experience requirements. These are:

a) a total of ten hours in free balloons with at least six flights under the supervision of a person holding a commercial pilot certificate with a free balloon rating.

These flights must include:

(i) two flights, each of at least one hour duration if a gas balloon is used, or of thirty minutes duration if a hot-air balloon with an airborne heater is used;

(ii) one ascent under control to 5,000 feet above takeoff point, in a gas balloon; or 3,000 above takeoff point in a hot-air balloon with an airborne heater;

(iii) one solo flight in a free balloon.

b) If a hot-air balloon without an airborne heater is used, you are required to make six flights in a free balloon under the supervision of a

commercial balloon pilot, including at least one solo flight.

7. The FAA likes to limit free balloon pilots, and if you take your flight test in a hot-air balloon with an airborne heater, your license will be so endorsed and you can only fly a hot-air balloon. This is under regulation 61.119, Free Balloon Ratings: Limitations.

Commercial Pilot Certificate   Subpart E—61.121 et seq.

1. To get a commercial pilot certificate with a free balloon rating, you must be at least eighteen years old.

2. You must be able to read, speak and understand English.

3. You must certify that you have no known medical defect that might make you unable to fly a free balloon. (You may take a Third-Class Medical, but it's not mandatory.)

4. You must pass a pretty advanced written test that covers the privileges, limitations and flight operations of a commercial pilot with a free balloon rating. It also includes knowledge of the use of aeronautical charts and a magnetic compass for free balloon navigation; recognition of weather conditions; how to obtain and use aviation weather forecasts in terms of free ballooning; free balloon flight and ground-instruction procedures and operating principles, including such emergency procedures as crowd control and protection, high-wind and water landings, and operations in the proximity of buildings and power lines.

5. You are required to have logged

flight instruction from an authorized flight instructor in specific pilot operations, plus an endorsement stating that you can perform the following operations competently as a commercial pilot:

a) inflation, rigging and mooring

b) ground- and flight-crew briefing

c) ascents

d) descents

e) landings

f) operation of airborne heater

g) emergency operations, including use of ripcord (may be simulated) and recovery from a terminal velocity descent if a balloon with an airborne heater is used.

6. According to regulation 61.137, aeronautical experience must include a total of at least thirty-five hours flight time as pilot, with:

a) twenty hours in free balloons*

b) ten flights in free balloons, including:
- six flights under supervision of a commercial free balloon pilot
- two solo flights

---

* This is where previous fixed or rotary wing flight time becomes valuable.

- two solo flights of at least two hours' duration if a gas balloon is used, or at least one hour's duration if a hot-air balloon with an airborne heater is used
- one ascent under control to more than 10,000 feet if a gas balloon is used, or 5,000 feet above take-off point if a hot-air balloon with an airborne heater is used.

c) If a hot-air balloon *without an airborne heater* is used, then the ten flights in free balloons should include:

- six flights under the supervision of a commercial free balloon pilot
- two solo flights.

7. A commercial free balloon pilot may act as pilot in command carrying persons or property for compensation or hire, and may give flight instruction in a free balloon if he or she holds a free balloon class rating.

8. Limitations of this category are found in regulation 61.141 of the FARs.

First Flight

Balloonist's Prayer
"I would like to rise very high, Lord;
Above my City,
Above the World,
Above Time;
I would like to purify my glance
and borrow Your Eyes."   Quoist

*T*he morning chorus is quick as the pale lemon lightening of a concealed sun lifts the shades of night into dawn. The headlights of your car seem to glow less brightly in the fading dark.

Almost there, you say to yourself.

Above the pasture there's a slight haze, and the meadow grass glistens with dew.

Despite the fact that this is what you've always secretly wanted to do, a slight chill stirs at the base of your spine. Old hands will recognize this as the "pucker factor."

You stop momentarily for a last check of the road map they sent you. Yes, this must be the turnoff, so you swing the wheel over and go off the highway down a dirt track. After about a quarter mile, you spot a truck parked in the field. You check for ditches and follow the track marks of the other vehicles.

"Glad you made it," someone says. "We're just about ready to unload."

You note the group at the end of the truck and a silhouette on board. The gondola. Venice of the skies! You think it seems rather small, if you're thinking at all; in fact, it seems almost fragile. Still, you don't let that worry you. People have been doing this for a couple of hundred years, and it's been remarkably safe, so you think positive thoughts instead.

You are about to enjoy the sport of the true "aristocrats" of our planet. Ballooning is a sport for those who have enough time and enough sense to enjoy what they're doing—those who realize that although their activities may only be a footnote in history, no one can steal their personal zest for life from them.

From the lofty perch provided by the gondola, you can experience the world of quivering-tailed deer, poking their noses delicately into human garbage, wondering what treasures they'll find, yet somehow distressed by these eruptions in their playground. You can enjoy the irritation-tinged interest of the hawks, who have seen human handiwork and recognize you as a beast that preys. The other birds, those who don't hunt for food, must speculate on what it is that mankind is up to this time. There's also the fox wondering how the hell you managed to find *him* from up there. He may even look up to measure the distance before mincing on his way.

First of all, you are told about the ground cloth. It is carefully laid down, and twigs, dead weeds and other natural debris are cleared from the area it will cover. Not everyone uses this lightweight blanket, but it will help keep dry that monstrous, unfurling envelope that will shortly bear you into the skies.

There's not much talking at the moment. Mostly people are working together at spreading the ground sheet out properly.

In the back of the truck is the gondola, the small bucket that hangs below the balloon and serves as the cockpit for the pilot and crew. The

Truck with gondola aboard, and a second balloon in middleground.
Predawn mists cling to the ground.

Tethered aerostat permits the tyro to practice gentle ascents and descents.

burner assembly, an anachronistic piece of technological furniture, rises above the wicker basket. It is still more efficient in terms of safety than anything modern technology has yet designed to replace it.

The gondola, which appears to carry the fabric of the balloon within itself, is brought over to the ground cloth and turned on its side. A big canvas bag is taken out of its interior and also placed on the ground cloth. People start taking out the fabric and carefully unfurl it. The person who's piloting wets a finger and holds it up in the air to determine the wind direction. You follow suit. The cool feeling makes you look for the wind, but nothing seems to be stirring. Everyone is looking around as the sky lightens. The lemon color deepens into a reddish pink while the stars start to fade away. A breath of wind stirs as the atmosphere quickens to the day and the sky reveals itself miraculously clear and clean. It's a beautiful day for your first flight.

Once the envelope is stretched out on the ground, the fabric is inspected for serious holes, including careful scrutiny of two special panels—the maneuvering vent and the rip panel. Someone comes over with a fan and, after a brief inspection, stands by for the pilot's okay. The morning quiet is broken by a sound resembling an outboard motor as the envelope is inflated.

People are holding the bottom end of the balloon.

The throat of the balloon is the mouth of it, and the skirt is the extra material around the end at 90 degrees to the entry point of the air.

"The skirt keeps the hot air going straight to the throat instead of being blown away."

You look at the balloon, which is now beginning to puff up. The material is laid out in specially cut long lines of fabric, sewn together at intervals. These seams are overlaid with strips of canvas which help distribute the load equally around the sphere. They carry some 90 percent of the overall weight of the outfit, while the fabric itself carries the rest and thus is never unduly stressed.

As you were arriving, you later learn, there was a crew briefing taking place. The briefing consists of an outline of what the day's flight mission is about, who's going in the gondola and chase car, which collects the balloons at the end of the flight, and who's going in the second and third balloons.

The weather forecast must be checked; sometimes the winds are likely to perk soon after dawn. Atmospheric activity requires heat, and, therefore, most activity at any particular time of day usually depends on the sun. Based on the weather, a probable landing site is selected. This may not be the actual one, but the area is usually big enough for the chase car.

The briefing ends with the pilot making sure that the ground crew knows the same telephone number. This is a mutually agreed-upon number on the ground which the crew of the chase car and balloon can call so that they know where the chase car has to go.

You begin to discover that there are set procedures with which everyone concurs, and that a lot more was going on than first met the eye.

The envelope's deflation port or maneuvering vent was secured, and its operating line checked to see that it ran smoothly to the gondola. The same thing was done to the ripping panel, a removable panel at the top end of the balloon, furthest away from the gondola. It was also secured with its Velcro fasteners, so that this line is also running free.

The ground-handling lines were laid out, so the balloon could be manhandled to prevent oscillation as it grew full and rose.

The fuel and burner systems were also checked. Fuel lines from tank to burner should be operating without leaks and should be switched on.

Because a balloon has only two controls—Up and Down—the checks are relatively straightforward. The fuel via the burners provides the Up control. The maneuvering vent and deflation system provide the Down control. Down control is also provided by cooling.

As the balloon gets larger, it's time for an inside inspection. The interior lines are supposed to be free and working properly. The Velcro fasteners of the deflation panel must be secure, and the telltale tab, with its four "never exceed" temperature markers, is carefully examined.

Modern fabric is extremely strong, closely woven, and treated to withstand the heat at the top of a balloon. It can handle temperatures as high as 250°F and even 350°F, for a short time. If the time limit permitted by the manufacturer is exceeded, or if the heat factor is too high, repairs must be made and much of the fabric replaced. The telltale tab openings inform the pilot whether allowable limits have been exceeded. If they have, there's no flight.

The object of the cold inflation is to provide for this inside inspection and for closer examination of the fabric itself, for any sizable holes that ought to be fixed before takeoff. If there are too many holes, or one or two big ones that would considerably decrease buoyancy as well as make the structure unsafe, it could ruin your whole day.

So that you know what the inside temperature is while you're flying, there's one other thing to do—hitch up the pyrometer, a thermocouple which indicates temperature at the top of the balloon where the hottest air gathers.

A powered inflator is used by all save the most procrustean of aeronauts, who still prefer to flop air into the throat for this stage of inflation.

Care is taken
in fitting together
fuel lines to prevent
in-flight emergency.

Portable powered fan
provides cold-air inflation.

When the checks are completed, you leave the modern fabric museum for the world outside. It is time for hot inflation.

The tanks are first installed in the gondola; the fuel lines are then matched up in the burner feed and tested for leaks and clear running. The flight burner and pilot light valves are closed while the plumbing is fitted together. Once fitted, the main tank valves are switched on and the lines—especially the joints—are tested for leakage.

Large leaks are found by the hissing noise they produce, together with a frostlike appearance at the loose fitting. Small leaks are more difficult, and you'll have to do a lot of sniffing around to find those. If in doubt, some saliva smeared over a suspected joint occasionally reveals the leak.

Next comes the flow test.

The pilot valve is opened and the pilot light ignited. The regulator is turned up to check whether gauge pressure changes with regulator adjustment and whether the burner is working properly. Poor flame control (a sputtering or smoky flame, or one which goes out) can mean dirt in the fuel feed or the burner jet itself. You can avoid dirt in the fuel lines if you always tape or cap the ends when the tanks are disconnected.

Before testing the blast valve, make sure the crew is well clear and that you're not going to burn up the fabric. A flame like the belch of a Bessemer converter shoots out when you test the blast valve. The first two or three times its blowtorchlike roar will make you jump.

If the system checks out okay, you proceed with the hot inflation. You keep the cold inflation going while you are hot inflating so that you don't end up with a hot spot, a blob of hot air that can quickly unbalance the aerostat if not dispersed.

As the blast valve is switched on, you're asked whether you'd mind holding onto the crown line (a line from the top of the balloon). What you'll do is to hold the balloon down with the crown line so that she rises slowly and you don't get a wobble as she goes up.

You take up your position at the head of the balloon. Soon there's a strain on the rope and you wonder how hard you ought to hold her down, since you might pull off the ripping panel. So you hold pretty hard, but not all that hard, and it seems about right. She rises very slowly, almost stately, as she expands to full size, and suddenly seems very big indeed.

Now the ground crew is holding the gondola down as inflation continues.

The burner is then switched off.

In a few more moments you'll have positive buoyancy, which means if you let go of the gondola, she'll hold her own weight just off the ground. If a little more heat is added, she'll rise.

The visual clue is slight, but an enormous amount of hot air is pouring into the balloon's envelope. Noise of the blast valve can disturb dogs and children.

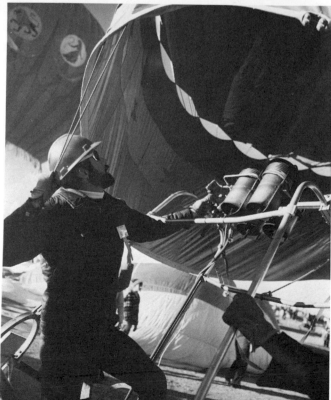

Pilot takes great care to aim carefully when hot-air inflation is taking place.

"We'll come down soon," says the pilot. "We don't want to travel too far. It takes longer for the pickup truck to fetch us. And we hope there isn't too much wind, as it makes for a bumpy landing."

A couple of points are selected *en route* as potential landing sites. The first would be fine, but it is rather far from a road, and the nearest house is nearly half a mile away. The next is rather small. It is bounded by wires and trees on three sides, except from the side you're approaching. You could get in, but it might be close with a windshift near the ground. This, too, is passed up.

There's also a belt of trees with a few houses on the side of a hill. In the distance is a long stretch of pasture.

"That's the spot," says the pilot, and we make ready for our approach and landing.

"Want to handle the descent?" offers the pilot.

"No thanks," you smile back.

"Watch the perspective of the ground very carefully as we come to it. If you decide to take up the sport, this is perhaps the most important thing to learn in making accurate landings. It's a visual clue you will always use."

You're not quite sure what to look for, and it's going to be two or three more landings before you discover the correct perspective for yourself.

He clears the telephone and power lines at the end of the field, and you're coming down. There's a light brush against a small hummock of weed, then a little bump, and for a moment she bounces forward, tilting, and you hold on. Then the ripping panel is pulled, and the envelope goes limp, melting before your eyes.

It's all over. You're in a different field, and all the magic is gone. You're back on earth, watching the wind lick lightly over the fabric as it settles on the ground.

"We can get out now," says the pilot. "If you'd straighten out the envelope, I'll go telephone the crew."

This is merely a thoughtful gesture, since there's hardly any work to be done; the wind's done it all for you. But you make a few things for yourself to do, so that you can look at your thoughts, evaluate the experience, and reexperience the wonder that was yours.

It'll be a memory you'll never forget—the joy of that exquisite harmony called aerostation.

PART III:

Weather and Navigation

Ballooning and the Weather

*H*ow the weather works is a fascinating subject, of interest to farmers, hunters, fishermen, tinkers and tailors and taxi drivers, military personnel and, of course, balloonists. Understanding it saves aeronauts a lot of time in misplaced optimism, as well as leaving bed early on a morning when there's not going to be any flying. Weather is also one of the easiest planetary sciences to learn about, yet it is consistently misunderstood by most people.

Weather is cited as a related factor in one fourth of all general aviation accidents and is a causal factor in many commercial airline crashes. The more pilots know about the way the weather works—whether dealing with wind sheer in the cockpit of a jet on short final, or waiting out a cold-front squall line—the better they can recognize the limitations of their own command abilities.

First of all, like everything else, the weather is always changing. The atmosphere is not stationary; its motion varies from nearly still to the rapid ragings of storms. Warm it, and the gases expand and rise. Let the air cool, and it will get denser and descend. The atmosphere is permeable to moisture and it can become dry. When it releases moisture it rains, snows, hails or there is fog.

The portion of the atmosphere that concerns us is the inner level of the mantle that surrounds the planet. This mantle of gases in which we live contains about three-quarters of the total mass of the earth's atmosphere. It is like a vast secondary sea which shrouds the planet's surface, extending from sea level to about 35,000 feet. Our weather forms here and is controlled by two principal factors—the sun and the earth's rotation.

The two outer levels of the atmosphere are the stratosphere and ionosphere. The stratosphere starts at 35,000 feet and extends upward approximately thirty miles. Jets, super jets and supersonics travel in this rarified atmosphere, up to altitudes of about 80,000 feet and sometimes more for certain military aircraft. The higher you go in the stratosphere, the warmer it gets and the more dangerous the hazard of radiation from the ultraviolet rays of the sun. Most of this radiation is absorbed by the strato-spheric ozone layer, a form of supersaturated oxygen which acts as a barrier. It is this layer that environmentalists fear may break down if the SST be-comes as ubiquitous as jumbo jets and aerosol spray cans.

The ionosphere is made up of very highly charged molecules and is important in radio communications, since various electrically charged levels enable radio signals to be bounced back to earth.

Back to the weather.

The sun and the earth's rotation act upon one another and the atmos-phere and determine the third factor in the weather—moisture. Moisture content of the local atmosphere is determined by the air's temperature, which is in turn controlled by the amount of local rotation.

Paradoxically, the atmosphere's temperature is not directly controlled by the sun. The sun's rays shine straight through the atmosphere without providing much heat until these rays are reflected back by the earth's surface. This means that different geophysical conditions will affect the climate. For example, less heat is returned to the atmosphere from a watery environment than from a fiery one such as a desert. This is why the Carib-bean islands, although tropical, are cooler in July each year than northern New York City, which adds to its problems with hot streets, huge air-conditioning units that vent waste heat into the air, and the pollution from numerous cars and trucks.

Another factor to consider is that the sun's rays don't strike the earth's surface equally all over. At the poles they come down at an oblique angle, and because the earth is tilted, there's not much heat available for absorp-tion. At the equator there is the opposite effect, since the sun strikes down at 90 degrees and consequently reradiation is greatest there.

This unequal heating coupled with rotation gives rise to a cyclical effect around the globe. To see how it works, let's stop the world for a moment and get rid of the rotation. Air heated at the equator rises—just like a balloon—because the air becomes less dense and therefore goes up. The air expands as it ascends, eventually losing all of its heat and becoming the same temperature as the surrounding air.

In the meantime, cooler air replaces the rising air. It moves in from the poles—since nature abhors a vacuum—then gets heated and rises. Meanwhile, the colder air has tumbled lower and lower until it settles

Sun's rays do not strike earth's surface equally, and rotational effect combines with unequal heating to produce weather movement. Air shown rising here at equator expands and virtually cools. Colder air flows in from north and south to replace this air, in turn being warmed, rising, and expanding.

around the poles, moves in, and the process is repeated. Okay, now start up the world again.

The earth's rotational forces extensively modify the normal pattern of heating and cooling. In addition, the presence of the sea or dry land also modifies local weather, as do sea currents of warmer water, like the ones which cause the mild British climate despite its northern latitude.

In the Northern Hemisphere, the rotational factor sets up a deflective motion of the air toward the right, if you view it from outside. In the Southern Hemisphere, it works in the opposite direction. What actually happens is very similar to what you do when you ferry-glide a canoe across a river by working against the current.

The best weather for ballooning is a day with light winds, clear skies and a long-distance horizon. If, on the other hand, you've set yourself a mission like crossing the continental United States or the Atlantic, you'll watch and pray for strong and steady winds.

The optimum conditions depend largely on what you want to do, but the real fun of aerostation is the actual flying. The experience becomes much more intimate with an early start, since you don't disturb people who might get agitated about your floating across their sky. And the animals and birds don't seem to mind, even if eccentric old gentlemen squawk "Peeping Tabithas!" as you waft by.

As discussed earlier, the FAA written examination requires you to know how the weather works in some detail.* You have to know about basic atmospheric circulation, the way air masses work and the types of clouds there are and why they form as they do. You also need to know about cold fronts, warm fronts, storms, and anything in between—you'll learn to be very pragmatic about published forecasts. And if you're really keen, you'll test the measure of the wind with a hand-held anemometer (which can be obtained from a good ship's chandler) and its direction with your compass.

For the examination, a certain amount of input is necessary. You're required to know how weather information is distributed, what buzz words or jargon are used to save time, and how accurate this information is in the first place. PIREPS—Pilot Reports—are a good source of information, since a pilot is reporting weather he or she has just flown through.

This is a service that few balloonists bother to use, one reason being that most are not in radio contact with the system. But every so often telephoned reports from balloonists—who actually fly in closer contact with weather than any other pilots—could show ground staff that pioneer-style aviators are still around, and can occasionally provide information that other pilots wouldn't be likely to know about.

Cold fronts are really spectacular. They are made up of air trying to expand. Of the movements between warm and cold air, the most interesting are the incoming cold fronts. They approach a warm blob of air with the patience of a tiger or like a lion stalking game. They are aggressive, trying to push up from underneath a small piece of warm air and climb over it too. Cold fronts are classified by their rate of movement—how fast they're going. The fast-moving cold front, more common in winter, whistles through the skies at a speed of about forty-five miles per hour and up to eighty miles per hour within the frontal system itself. This is no weather in which to be ballooning unless you want to try for a distance record and hope for the very best of luck.

Slow-moving cold fronts are cloud makers. If the air ahead of them is unstable and moist, there will be a build-up of heavy cumulus clouds. If the air is drier and more stable, stratiform clouds will develop. During the summer, cold fronts produce thunder clouds, also known as cumulonimbus.

When cold fronts eventually catch up with warm fronts, there is the possibility of what is called an occluded front developing. An occluded front occurs when a cold and warm front become adjacent to one another,

---

* The classic book is *Weather Flying*, by Robert N. Buck. A fine read.

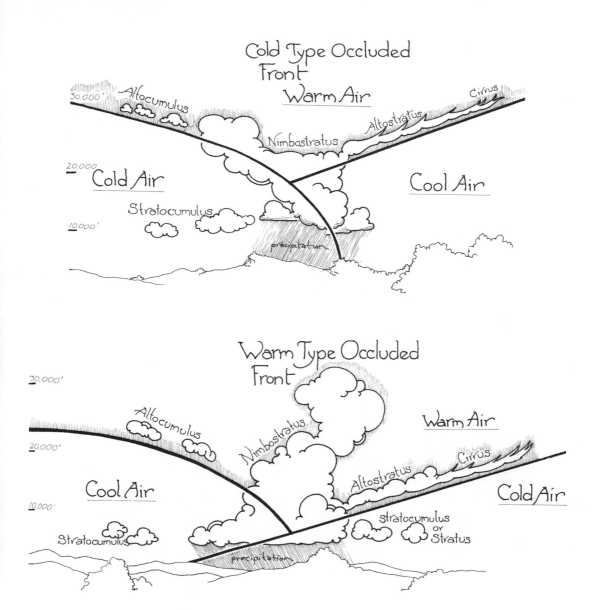

but both are still subject to their own centrifugal reaction, causing their edges to flow outward. Thus, an occluded front can be either cold or warm, depending on what type of front develops at the edge of the low-pressure system. In terms of the sort of weather you can expect, an occluded front usually means widespread rain and clouds with poor visibility. During the winter, icing is probable in clouds in almost all types of frontal systems.

A warm front forms when a mass of cold air retreats before a warm air mass. Because it is less dense than cold air, a wedge of hot air will tend to rise on a slight incline over the cold air. The front moves slowly forward at about fifteen miles per hour, squeezing the cold air forward in its path. As the warm air rises, it cools, and this in turn condenses its moisture content, forming clouds. Under certain conditions a warm front will produce cirrus clouds at 30,000 feet and even higher. As the front develops, cirrostratus clouds are added, followed by altostratus and finally nimbostratus, mushy clouds full of moisture. A warm front may be preceded by cirrus clouds as much as 600 miles from its center, and heavy rains are likely about 200 miles ahead of the actual ground front. Warm fronts tend to cover rather large areas of land and sea.

From the point of view of pilots, warm fronts spell clouds and rain. In addition to cumulonimbus clouds, low-level stratus clouds and fog—due to high humidity—are also probable. This is definitely not good weather for flying balloons.

There is one other type of front—the stationary front, which as its name implies stands still or shows little movement. Stationary fronts occur when two adjacent air masses have equal pressure. The weather is similar but less intense than a warm front.

On a weather map, fronts are depicted by lines to which little arrowheads or semicircles are attached. The areas from which they are centered are marked either with an H (High) or L (Low). Within these lines are additional lines, rather like the gradients on a map, that show changes in pressure. Their proper name is isobar(s). When there are wide spaces between the isobars, the pressure gradient is small, and winds tend to be light—usually good weather for ballooning. When they are tightly packed together, on the other hand, you may expect strong winds.

Air tends to move inward on itself and counterclockwise around low-pressure systems. It moves clockwise around high-pressure systems. In the Southern Hemisphere, the direction of air movement is reversed.

Since you will encounter the wind sooner or later while ballooning, you should know how it works. Wind is simply air in motion. The reason the air moves is twofold—the rotation of the earth and nature's dislike of vacuums. Winds occur because of the movements of the different air masses and their interactions with each other around the sphere. The earth's spin allows for a reasonable prediction of local systems, such as the trade winds in the tropics, the northeast trades to about thirty degrees north latitude, the prevailing westerlies to about sixty degrees north latitude, and the polar easterlies at the North Pole. Wind, by the way, is always reported *from* the direction it is coming from; an east wind is one *from* the east.

High-altitude winds tend to move pretty close to the isobars, or pressure gradients. Lower winds, because of friction between the air mass and the planet's surface, tend to move more erratically, usually across or diagonal to the gradient lines. Over water, where there is less friction, there's usually only about a ten-degree difference between upper and lower winds. But over a mountain chain, such as the Rockies, you may find a thirty-degree to fifty-degree directional difference between upper and lower winds, that is, between surface wind and winds 6,000 feet above ground level (AGL). The greatest difference occurs between the surface and 3,000 feet. This is worth remembering, since you can occasionally make this information work for you.

Another useful bit of lore about winds is that easterly winds tend to decrease with altitude: above 20,000 feet, most winds are westerlies. North winds back to the west, and winds from the south tend to veer.

Air temperature drops at a rate of 2°C (3.6°F) every 1,000 feet upward, with a further drop caused by the expansion of the air as it rises. This gives an overall drop in temperature of around 3°C (5.5°F) per 1,000 feet.

In addition to this rate of cooling, which might be termed "standard," there is also indirect cooling due to the air's moisture content. And since there is always some moisture in the atmosphere—which is why it is possible to precipitate water in a desert using a solar still (a device used to distill water out of the atmosphere)—sufficient cooling will produce rain, mist, snow or fog. The point is that the air can only retain a certain amount of moisture at any time, and this quantity depends upon its temperature. Power-plane pilots are particularly aware of this and study the relationship between moisture and temperature, a ratio known as the dew point. When temperature and dew point are close together, the possibility of carburetor icing is enhanced and with it, motor shut down.

When temperature and dew point are within 4°F of each other, you can usually predict fog. Fog is really stratiform clouds within fifty feet of the planet's surface. The ingredients for fog include high humidity, a dew point close to actual temperature, and a very light surface wind. You will not find fog developing in conditions of moderate wind, and without any wind at all, fog simply breaks out in patches, usually in hollows or areas protected from air movement. When temperature and dew point are 2°F or less from each other, fog is certain; provided there is a light wind to help "brew" it, you won't be flying that day.

Ground fog—radiation fog—will normally be burned off as the sun rises. Formed by the cooling of air near the ground, which causes temperature and dew point to approach each other, it can occur when the skies are clear.

Advection fog is common in coastal regions and is formed when warm, humid air flows over a cold surface. The warm air is cooled by the ground, and once again, as temperature and dew point move together, fog occurs.

Unlike most kinds of fog, advection fog may contain winds of up to twelve knots, which cause it to thicken. If the winds are more than fifteen knots, the fog lifts from the surface and forms a low layer of stratus clouds. Advection fogs which form over the sea and are then blown over land are known as sea fogs.

Another fog associated with water is the so-called steam fog. This happens when cold air moves over water that is warmer than the air. You may have seen this happen on a summer morning when "steam" appears to form over a small pond or lake.

What happens is that the relatively intense evaporation from the water into the cold air above it causes the water vapor to condense—thus, instant fog. Fog may also be caused by excessive rain, which sends the humidity soaring, or when rain evaporates on reaching the ground, which occurs more frequently at night than during the day.

Finally, there are fogs that break out on mountains and hills, caused by the flow of moist air moving *up* the slope. The moisture in the air condenses as it cools—temperature and dew point approach each other. Mountain or hill fogs need winds to push them up the slope in order to form.

In addition to fog, there is also haze. Haze is caused by fine particles of dust suspended in the atmosphere. Smoke has an effect similar to haze in terms of visibility but is produced mostly from industrial sources. The term smog originally applied to a mixture of smoke and fog, but today the term applies to any heavy concentration of air pollution. Another term you may come across during your weather briefing is "smaze"—smoke and haze—which also means poor visibility.

Safe ballooning means understanding the weather forecast. Flight Service Stations have weather information that was unknown to early aeronauts. By understanding how the weather works, you will soon be able to make reasonably informed and accurate weather predictions of your own. A proper weather briefing, together with the long-range forecast, is where you start.

Since you will do much of your flying early in the morning, the evening TV weather is a good place to begin. Augment this by using the Pilot's Automatic Telephone Weather Answering Service (PATWAS) or the Transcribed Weather Broadcast (TWEB), which is available in most areas of the United States.

Once you've got a general overview, you can further check out what's happening weatherwise by calling your nearest Flight Service Station. This costs money occasionally, if you have to call long distance, but it is essential.

In order to obtain a useful weather briefing, you need some knowledge of how the system works. You need to know the right questions to get the right answers. Before getting a weather briefing, have an area chart and a paper and pencil in front of you so that you can take notes. You might also draw a rough sketch map of your area.

First get the synoptic weather. This is a weather-data summary based on the most up-to-the-minute information available. A few terminal forecasts will help flesh out the picture, and then you'll need to know the winds aloft. From this you will be able to gauge the accuracy of the general overview you got earlier. You will also be interested in any Significant Meteorological Advisories (called SIGMETS), Advisories for Light Aircraft (called AIRMETS) and Notices to Airmen (called NOTAMS).

> *Coded weather sequence reports provide detail of local atmospheric conditions. Details include reporting station, cloud coverage, wind, local pressure, and visibility.*

```
    SA NEAR WEST 051903
BUF M50⊕15  121/55/25/1710/987
ROC 40⊕800E25⊕12+  139/58/27/1209/993→ROC↘ 5/2 5/4
ART
UCA 250-⊕20+  147/54/24/0505/E996
ELM
BGM 250-⊕45  149/52/19/2211/994
POU 120⊕E25⊕20+  166/58/20/1706/001
SWF E20⊕030 55/18/1502/001
BFD 65⊕E25⊕15+  128/53/28/1910/987
DUJ 5⊕E25⊕15+  127/57/28/1710G20/988
IPT WWPVEPPBWTZ  153/56/30/1513/998
AVP  15⊕E25⊕25+  150/54/23/2109/996/BINOVC
PSB E25⊕10+  140/55/28/1815/991FEW CU
AOO 10⊕⊕E25⊕20/149/54/28/1810/994→AOO↘4/6
RDG E15⊕15+  58/30/1407/002
HAR 10⊕⊕E15⊕15  171/56/27/2010/002→HAR↘4/3
ABE 16⊕⊕E22⊕25  171/53/30/1309/003
PNE 10⊕⊕E20⊕10 58/15/1908
MRB 10⊕⊕E20⊕20 162/35/32/1405/001



03



    SA NEAR SOUTH 051904
MIV E25⊕7+  186/58/38/E1608/007
ACY 250-⊕8  183/54/34/1509/007→ACY↘5/8 5/9
ILG E25⊕030 171/56/27/1808/004/ →ILG↘ 5/1
DCA 5⊕E120⊕10 169/58/30/1605/003→DCA↘3/59 4/50 4/56 5/3 5/10
SBY E10⊕10 176/54/33/1012/005
CHO 25⊕E40⊕10R- 170/53/47/0000/003
RIC E45⊕4R  166/52/46/0904/002→RIC↘3/2 4/12
PHF E60⊕100⊕7R-- 52/45/0708/001→PHF↘2/2 4/9
ORF 5⊕E100⊕6R-- 159/55/47/0808/000
```

SIGMETS tell you about potentially dangerous weather. They apply to all pilots and will normally include details of thunderstorms, severe turbulence, hail and icing. Also included will be notes about squall lines, dust storms and hurricanes. This is no weather to go ballooning.

AIRMETS are about weather likely to be dangerous to light aircraft. They include details of moderate icing, moderate turbulence, winds of forty knots or more within 2,000 feet of the ground. Also included in AIRMETS are details concerning decreasing visibility and lowering ceilings, especially in or around mountainous areas.

NOTAMS contain general information of interest to pilots, such as radio beacons shut down for repair and closed airports.

To put all this information together for you, the weather briefer uses a surface-analysis chart, a weather-depiction chart and a radar-summary chart. More and more FSS weather bureaus are using satellite charts these days, and if a recent one is available, you'll have the benefit of that, too.

The surface chart shows the highs and lows in the area and plots frontal activity. The weather-depiction chart denotes the local area as part of an overall weather system, so that you have a better idea of how accurate the forecast is going to be in your area. The weather-depiction chart will indicate areas marginal or below VFR (Visual Flight Rules). As a student pilot, you will tend to get a better briefing if you identify yourself as such. The radar chart shows medium to heavy rains and any thunderstorm activity picked up by the radar set.

For your flight planning, you will want a full sequence of probable weather conditions at your starting point, and given the wind, some idea of what the weather will be where you are going to land. (In light winds the weather at your start and finish points will be almost the same.) Thus wind is an important factor—too much of it and you won't be flying. Wind forecasts are given to 9,000 feet only, and you'll need to ask for higher-altitude forecasts if you need them. You'll be told about any significant SIGMETS, AIRMETS and NOTAMS.*

It is well worth the effort to visit a Flight Service Station (FSS), since you can see firsthand how this information is collected and dispensed. There are several teletype machines that spew out reams of data on the hour every hour. There are large photocopy-type machines that produce charts, and, of course, the telephones are going much of the time.

Airports issue updated weather forecasts every hour on the hour. A

---

* If you're not—ask for them, and why they were not volunteered. They're supposed to be given.

*Where the clouds are, their shapes, their identities,
including abbreviation and code symbols.*

special code comprised of letters and symbols is used for abbreviating the information they contain. The first three letters in each forecast identify the issuing station. If the report is special—which means there has been a fairly dramatic change in the local weather—the letters SP, together with an indication of the time of issuance, are added to the three-letter code.

The next piece of information is details of the sky and the ceiling. The sky above the issuing station is described as clear when there is less than one-tenth cloud cover. Between one-tenth and six-tenths it is described as "scattered"; "broken" between six-tenths and nine-tenths, and finally, "overcast" when more than nine-tenths is covered. If, as occasionally occurs, there are several cloud layers, then the forecast will note the type of cloud cover and at what height it occurs. One might find scattered stratus at a ceiling of 4,000 feet, with broken cumulus at 8,000 feet and finally overcast at 12,000 feet.

Next comes current visibility and actual local weather, with letters identifying any visual obstructions. Sea-level atmospheric pressure is quoted next, in millibars, followed by the issuing station's temperature and dew point. This is followed by the local wind, its direction (in degrees) and speed (in knots). The current local altimeter setting is quoted in inches of mercury. Just in case you don't understand it, the sea-level pressure and the altimeter readouts both omit the first figure for brevity.

Occasionally there may be additional remarks. At some airports you'll find a figure quoting runway visual range and coded pilot reports (PIREPS) noted before the remarks. PIREPS are a useful source of information since they are filed by pilots. Such items as the tops of cloud formations and notes about turbulence and icing may be found here. As a balloon pilot, it is unlikely you'll have anything to report very often, but if you do note something unusual—even a flock of geese settling at an airport—file it when you come down. It may be of use to another air traveler.

Runway visual range (coded as VR in sequence reports) is a measurement of visibility near the touchdown point on a runway. It is useful to instrument flying pilots and is measured by a device called a transmissometer. This machine measures the intensity of runway lights or visual contrast of various targets near the touchdown area.

It is unlikely that you'll be using the radio in your balloon much of the time, but if you are looking to break a distance record, it is worth noting the availability of en-route weather reports. Started in 1972 on the West Coast, en-route weather advisory service (EWAS) is planned to be operative across the nation using forty-four stations. A weather frequency of 122.0 MHz is specially set up to get you up-to-the-minute advisories and PIREPS from a weather station near you.

A final word about weather. Even if the sky is clear and visibility unlimited, it is wise to get a weather briefing. It's your responsibility as an aviator. Part 91.5 of the FARs states very clearly that "each pilot in command shall, before beginning a flight, familiarize himself with all available information concerning that flight." Weather is very much a part of the information you need to fly safely. Besides, having an accurate weather picture the night before may prevent you from disturbing your beauty sleep the next morning!

Balloon Navigation

"Then you have discovered the means
    of guiding a balloon?"
"Not by any means, that is a Utopian idea."
"Then, you will go—"
"Withersoever Providence wills . . ."
Five Weeks in a Balloon
Jules Verne, 1869.

*I*f you've ever sailed, you will enjoy navigating balloons. Here you are hoisted above the horizon, able to see the very pattern of the earth. And if the sky is calmer than the sea—and it has to be if you want to go ballooning—you get an immeasurably more comfortable ride. If only they'd design one like a ship, you will think to yourself.

Navigation from a balloon operates the way you always wish it would in a car when you can't find the exit from the thruway that will save you fifty minutes on the way home. The ground is all spread out before you, and if it doesn't seem to agree with your road map, then you'd better get an aviation sectional chart of your area.

The drawback of the sectional chart is that its scale is better read from 5,000 feet or higher. You can supplement this chart with a variety of maps, such as those produced by the U.S. Geological Survey, 1200 South Eads St., Arlington, Virginia 22202.

Actually, what happens is that you begin to learn your whole area— first within a radius of four or five miles, then a bit further. But it's always in a 360-degree pattern, since the winds will take you hither and yon. You learn to check the winds rather carefully, since you obviously don't want to fly over a built-up or industrial area, where landing places may be difficult to find and where accidents have more potential to occur.

Since you are in low flight in a balloon, it is better to learn how wind currents change your flight path, particularly where the wind blows across the brow of a hill. Even the fact that a particular hill is wooded or open can produce variation.

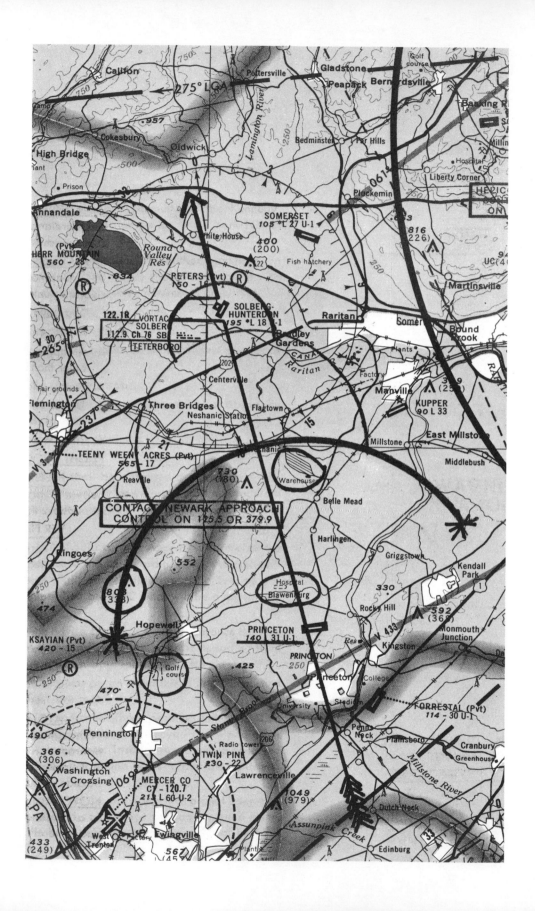

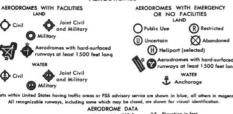

WASHINGTON
AERONAUTICAL SYMBOLS

AERODROMES

WASHINGTON
SECTIONAL AERONAUTICAL CHART
SCALE 1:500,000

Lambert Conformal Conic Projection Standard Parallels 33°20′ and 38°40′
Topographic data corrected to July 1971

10 TH EDITION corrected to include airspace amendments effective September 16, 1971
and all other aeronautical data received by August 16, 1971
Consult appropriate NOTAMS and Flight Information
Publications for supplemental data and current information.
This chart will become OBSOLETE FOR USE IN NAVIGATION upon publication of
the next edition scheduled for MARCH 30, 1972

PUBLISHED IN ACCORDANCE WITH INTER-AGENCY AIR CARTOGRAPHIC COMMITTEE
SPECIFICATIONS AND AGREEMENTS APPROVED BY:
DEPARTMENT OF DEFENSE FEDERAL AVIATION ADMINISTRATION DEPARTMENT OF COMMERCE

AERODROMES WITH FACILITIES
LAND
Civil Joint Civil and Military
Military
Aerodromes with hard-surfaced runways at least 1500 feet long
WATER
Civil Joint Civil and Military
Military

AERODROMES WITH EMERGENCY OR NO FACILITIES
LAND
Public Use Restricted
Uncertain Abandoned
Heliport (selected)
Aerodromes with hard-surfaced runways at least 1500 feet long
WATER
Anchorage

Airports within United States having traffic areas or FSS advisory service are shown in blue, all others in magenta.
All recognizable runways, including some which may be closed, are shown for visual identification.

AERODROME DATA
CT – 118.3	Control Tower and primary frequency	INTNL CT – 118.3 ATIS – 124.9 03 L 92 U-2 Airport of entry DF
NFCT – 118.3	Non-Federal Control Tower and primary frequency	
ATIS – 124.9	Automatic Terminal Information Service	

03 Elevation in feet
L Lighting (see below)†
92 Length of longest runway in hundreds of feet
S Normally sheltered take-off area

U-1: Indicates aeronautical advisory station licensed to operate
on 122.8; U-2 on 123.0; U-3 on 123.05; U-4 on 122.85; U-5 on 122.95

† – L – Lighting in operation Sunset to Sunrise.
*L – Lighting available Sunset to Sunrise only on request (by radio call, letter, phone, telegram, circling the field etc.).
(L) – Lighting in operation part of the night and on request, or not operating thereafter.
When facility or information is lacking, the respective character is replaced by a dash.

RADIO AIDS TO NAVIGATION
VHF OMNI RANGE (VOR) VORTAC VOR-DME
Radiobeacon, nondirectional (homing) Other Facilities LF/MF Radio Range
Continuous line indicates "N" quadrant

Shadow box indicates Standard FSS freqs 122.1R 122.6 123.6 and 255.4
MARTINSBURG
206 114.0 NGP
Underline indicates no voice on this frequency
379T 122.2 — Non Standard FSS freqs available

Plain box with freq indicates less than all Standard FSS freqs available
123.6 or 122.6 — All Standard FSS freqs except 123.6 available
123.6 available
Controlling Area FSS
WASHINGTON
Plain box without freq indicates no Standard FSS freq available
CLEVELAND
ARTCC Remoted Sites — — Toledo

AIRSPACE INFORMATION
Prohibited, Restricted, Warning and Alert Area
CZ – Control Zone
TA – Transition Area
Control zones with in which fixed-wing special VFR Flight is prohibited.
Parachute Jumping Area (See part 4 of AIM for details)
Low Altitude Federal Airways are indicated by center line
092° V 3
Intersection
Arrows are directed toward facilities which establish intersection
The limits of controlled airspace are shown by tint bands (Vignette) and are color-coded in blue and magenta
Floor 700 feet above surface
Floor 1200 feet above surface
Floors other than 700 feet or 1200 feet above surface 2000 2000 MSL
Only the controlled and reserved airspace effective below 18,000 feet MSL are shown on this chart.

AIRPORT TRAFFIC AREAS
Federally operated control tower
FSS
DAYTON CT –119.9
1008 L 70
Non-Federal control tower
MARTIN NFCT – 119.2
556 L 70
Other Airport (no traffic area, no FSS at airport)
SOMERSET
1540 L 37
Hours of operation of tower, if not continuous, are included with tower frequencies

MISCELLANEOUS
Obstruction below 1000 feet AGL
UC 921 (260)
Obstruction 1000 feet and higher AGL
1520 (1210)
Group Obstruction 745 (456) or 1047 (1025)
Isogonic Line (1965 VALUE) — 2°W —
UC (Under Construction) or reported, position and elevation unverified.
Numerals without parenthesis indicate elevation above sea level of top
Numerals with parenthesis indicate the height of the structure above ground
Power Transmission Line
Rotating Light Fl
Rotating Light (with course lights and code) 17
Marine Light 12 MON 112.6 CHARL
Visual Flight Routes through mountain passes.

CONTOUR INTERVAL
500 feet
Intermediate contours shown at 250 feet

500 250
Basic Intermediate

HIGHEST TERRAIN elevation is
4050 feet
located at 38°33′N – 78°24′W

Critical elevation — 4254
Approximate elevation — x3200
Doubtful locations are indicated by omission of the point locator (dot or "x")

MAXIMUM TERRAIN ELEVATIONS
Maximum Terrain elevation figures, centered in the area completely bounded by ticked lines of latitude and longitude, are represented in THOUSANDS and HUNDREDS of feet BUT DO NOT INCLUDE ELEVATIONS OF VERTICAL OBSTRUCTIONS.

3100 feet — 31

CONVERSION OF ELEVATIONS
FEET (Thousands) 0 2 4 6 8 10 12 14 16 18 20 22 24 26 28 30
METERS (Thousands) 0 1 2 3 4 5 6 7 8 9

Published at Washington, D.C.
U.S. Department of Commerce
National Oceanic and Atmospheric Administration
National Ocean Survey

PRICE 80 CENTS

Outer cover of Sectional Aeronautical Chart

Map shows: Forecast wind direction from Princeton to Solberg-Hunterdon Airport. First arc is used to determine actual flight path with circles around the more obvious check points (clockwise: golf course, an obstruction rising to 803 feet probably a TV tower, hospital grounds, and some warehouses and railroad tracks.) The second arc comes into play at a later point in the flight, while the third represents the final portion. Most navigation for local flying is done by routine eyeballing and—very frequently—a Geodesic Survey map with a smaller scale.

You'll also become familiar with the changing temperature of the air. It's rather like swimming in the sea in the summer; you find different pockets of colder and warmer water. This makes a difference in your flight path.

Because you will seldom be moving much faster than a horse can gallop, changes in scenery—and position on your chart, if you want to track your course—are pleasantly slow, thanks to your additional height above the ground. For this reason it is rather difficult to get really lost. By the time you're ready to move further out of your home territory, following your progress on a map will be second nature. You'll also be able to experience the great satisfaction that reading a map can give.

Even if you've never read a surface (topographical) map before, it's really very easy. The map is a pictorial representation of the ground, which tries to reproduce the contours of the planet's surface in figures, colors and lines.

One way to learn to read such a map easily is to take a small section of it and make a sideview three-dimensional model from the figures. You can do this because maps shrink the surface; in order to contain a wide area into a small piece of paper they are scaled down. Sectionals, which are specially produced maps for people who fly, are highly accurate renderings. Their scale is 1:500,000, which means approximately eight statute miles to one inch.*

Sectional maps are referred to by the area they cover. They normally have a north and south half. Underneath the area name you'll find the type of chart (in this case "sectional"), its scale (1:500,000), and a detail of the type of projection used. The projection describes the process by which a part of a spherical surface is shown on a flat surface. The type now favored for middle latitudes is the Lambert Conformal Conic projection, which is jargon for saying that a straight line on one of these charts closely represents a great circle route—the quickest way of getting from A to B when you're on a sphere. The chart also tells when it will be out of date and you'll need to get a new one.

Sectionals are also useful for indicating the location of TV towers. They do not necessarily tell you about power lines, but it's wise to keep up to date.

---

* It is a good idea for balloon pilots to know about nautical miles. These are longer than statute miles—6,076.10 feet, a distance equal to one-sixtieth of one degree at the earth's equator. One statute mile measures 5,280 feet and is derived from the Roman measure of one thousand paces, which was—approximately 1,620 yards. (Taller soldiers take longer paces, goes the saying, which may be why the United States and Britain both measure 1,760 yards to their mile.)

Your chart, in order to depict a section of the sphere, uses parallel lines going from north to south and from east to west. The north-south lines are called meridians and are expressed in terms of longitude. The east-west lines are known as parallels of latitude. The north-south lines are measured east or west of Greenwich, just outside Old London, and now a part of the Greater London Area. Greenwich is zero degrees. The equator is the other zero line, from which one measures north or south.

Navigation and Flight Planning

One of the most important things you need to know in planning a flight are the wind conditions. The weathermen can give you this information. The degrees of wind shift will become apparent as you ascend, and you can estimate what your course is likely to be. At this stage it is only approximate, so simply draw a very faint line on the chart indicating what your projected track is likely to be. This depends to some extent on your understanding of the weather.

Now check this against the chart (or map) that you will be using. Will you be crossing any extra-hilly places? How much extra gas will this require? (There may be places where you'll need to calculate for additional burning to make good downdrafts—off the sides of hills, for example, when the wind is blowing in the wrong direction.)

Look again at the chart. Where will you land? How far could you go? How far do you want to go?

You don't need to be a daredevil. The whole point about ballooning is that it is a safe sport—*you* make it safe.

All flying machines in the United States are required to carry a compass. These are normally rather cheap items made for power boats, automobiles and regular aircraft. Since weight is not as important a factor in balloons as in regular aircraft and gliders, it is worthwhile to get an inexpensive ship's compass which has compensating weights.

The compass should have a special box in which it is stowed for flight. To set the compass, it will be necessary to secure the balloon to a tether and then swing it to correct the compensating magnets. The procedure is as follows:

1. Find an area reasonably free of power lines where a balloon flight—and tethering—is secure from the wind.

2. Inflate the balloon and once equilibrium is established, secure the tether line to a post or ground anchor.

3. Check the master compass—used on the ground—against the ship's compass on the ground.

4. Install the ship's compass in the balloon, and recheck against the master compass.

5. Raise the balloon. Check at ten-foot intervals to thirty feet. Adjust as necessary. (It is usual to check out the four cardinal points, north, south, east and west. The balloon is rotated by its drag lines.)

If you want to stay with the compass supplied by the balloon maker, simply swing it, and use a paper chart which is placed by the compass indicating the degrees of error at the cardinal points.

Compasses work by telling you where magnetic north is—the northernmost segment of the planet's magnetic field, where the lines of force meet. This is not true north, but an imaginary point where the North Pole ought to be. As a result of this there are variations. Sometimes the compass points east when it means west, and vice versa. It's all explained on your navigation chart. And for the balloonist this is not really important anyway. Still, you might as well know about the earth's magnetic field—it's the sort of tricky question you could be asked on the FAA exam, and it's good to know the answer.

Even the smallest atoms have a field of force, created by the solidification of energy that is involved when solid particles form. The force with which individual particles cohere, and the directional force they exert upon one another, causes a magnetic field to arise, in much the same way that we can create electricity by winding a turbine very fast.

This field of force has two polarities, north and south, which do not match the theoretical north and south of our planet. Consequently, maps drawn in relation to theoretical north have to be reinterpreted by readers to compensate for the difference between compass (magnetic or centrifugal) north and planetary north.

Our planet's magnetic North Pole moves around a bit from year to year. It's a free spirit, though not so free that one cannot forecast its yearly variations. Therefore it is necessary to make miniscule adjustments on the map. (The speed of a balloon is so slow, however, that it really isn't worth the bother.)

If the compass is your prime navigational instrument, the flight computer is a good second one to have. While the compass lets you know in which direction you are traveling, the flight computer (a circular slide rule device) allows you to rapidly make numerous calculations that refine this information.

These computers were originally designed to enable bomber pilots to navigate efficiently. But wartime computers were ungainly and cumbersome and came in large wooden boxes. Someone had the bright idea of turning them into circular slide rules—and the handy computer was born.

The most common type is the E6B; the more favored is the CR series which is smaller and easier to handle. Both kinds of computers have two sides. One side has numbers all over it—the slide rule part—and is designed to help you work out questions of time and distance, conversions from statute to nautical miles (it's always easier to work in nautical miles), and any multiplication or division problem. The other side has to do with wind triangles and is more for power pilots, but it is still useful for working out where you are actually going instead of your projected course. Today, electronic calculators are moving to the fore.

Since you're supposed to know about this for the FAA written exam, it is a good idea to learn to use the wind triangle part of a computer. The wind side consists of a sliding grid, a true index, and an azimuth circle that rotates through 360 degrees. At the center is a transparent portion on which you can write with a soft pencil; it has a dot or grommet in the middle. Wind direction is set in by rotating the azimuth circle. By checking against your chart, you can determine just what the wind is doing—if it is blowing differently from the forecast, and if so, by how much. (Obviously, if you stick your head over the side of the gondola every so often and check out your checkpoints, you'll get the same answer.)

Let's look now at our overall scheme of things.

First of all, we've checked with the Flight Service Station (FSS) for the weather and have received the details of what's presently happening (their information is at least one hour out of date) and what's likely to happen. At this point it's worthwhile to remember that forecasting these days is approximately 75 percent accurate in prediction of such types of weather as the passage of warm fronts and slow-moving cold fronts up

COMPRESSIBILITY CORRECTION

PRESSURE ALTITUDE	F CORRECTION FACTORS FOR TAS CALIBRATED AIRSPEED IN KNOTS							
	200	250	300	350	400	450	500	550
10,000 FT.	1.00	1.00	.99	.99	.98	.98	.97	.97
20,000 FT.	.99	.98	.97	.97	.96	.95	.94	.93
30,000 FT.	.97	.96	.95	.94	.92	.91	.90	.89
40,000 FT.	.96	.94	.92	.90	.88	.87	.87	.86
50,000 FT.	.93	.90	.87	.86	.84	.84	.84	.84

USE CALIBRATED AIRSPEED AND PRESS. ALT. TO OBTAIN F FACTOR. MULTIPLY F FACTOR BY **TAS** TO OBTAIN THE **TAS** CORRECTED FOR COMPRESSIBILITY.

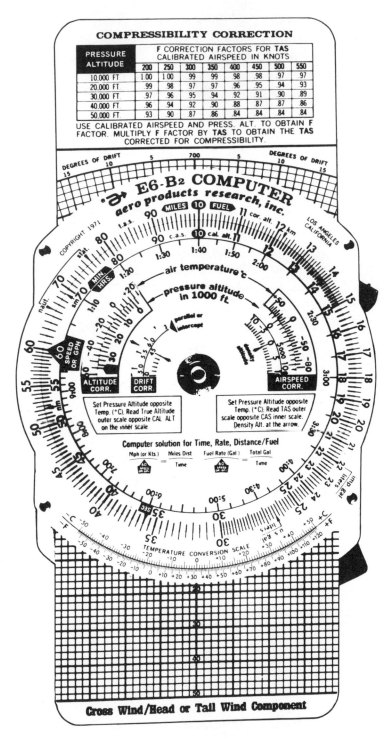

The E6B flight computer—more useful to power flight and gliding specialists.

to twelve hours in advance, plus or minus five hours. And fast-moving cold fronts with their associated squall lines can be forecast up to ten hours in advance, plus or minus a couple of hours.

So you've got the weather. Winds will be light, says the forecast.

On your chart, shade in the area in which you will probably be flying. Don't forget that winds change direction as you ascend, and if there's going to be some wind at sea level, chances are quite good that there will be more wind at higher altitudes. The forecast gives the winds up to 9,000 feet. Remember, if for some reason you want to know the winds at a higher level, simply ask for them.

Now you know approximately where you'll be flying. The next thing to do is to note some potential checkpoints on your route. This is quite easy to do. It may be a group of buildings, a solitary building, a railroad track or a river with a bridge going over it—any object featured on the chart can be used. Take a rule, preferably with a gauge representing inches to the mile and appropriate for your sectional, and measure off with a compass little arcs, spaced about two miles from each other and about a mile long. Do this lightly with a soft pencil. Spread these arcs out over an angle of about 80 degrees, the center of which is along the line of the forecast sea-level wind. (Note: If the wind at 3,000 feet is blowing in a markedly different direction, think again about flying—and check the wind speed.) This gives you a spread of 40 degrees on each side of you and is the area in which you are most likely to travel. Were you to draw a line parallel with the center at the end of the furthest arc, you would have a path across the map, like a large road.

In addition to looking for checkpoints directly ahead of you, also look for checkpoints to each side. This will enable you to tell how your actual flight over the ground is shaping up while you go along. It's sometimes useful to mark projected time on the chart. (In the cockpit of an airplane it's easier to write it down on a sheet of paper, and you can do that if you enjoy bookkeeping. The main point about ballooning is being able to fly without the bookkeeping, since that way it's so much more fun when you arrive.) Checkpoints should be recognized from the chart, since they give you an idea of just how long it'll take for the pickup truck to fetch you when you finally land, and enable you to tell the driver exactly where to find you.

Some balloonists use radios, and they can be quite useful: the FAA apparently thinks so too, and includes a question about VORs in the private pilot's written examination. VOR stands for Very High Frequency Omni-

Directional Range and refers to a radio beacon that permits you to dial its magnetic course bearing from your cockpit; if you center the needle, it will lead you to the beacon. This is not much use to balloonists, since they are at the mercy of the wind, but it is worth knowing about, and the use of radios is discussed in more detail in the next chapter.

The best reason to become a skilled navigator is that it removes certain areas of uncertainty from your mind, enabling you to spend more time enjoying the flight. And once you're proficient, it's just another item you can enjoy doing automatically while you marvel at the world below. Another great advantage is that you will always be at home, wherever you are. You're never in unfamiliar territory with a chart or map, and you'll be able to forecast the vagaries of the wind as it spins up hill and down dale.

The Corps of Engineers is a good source for maps, and a number of their surveys have produced excellent material. The sectional is also good, and it is in standard use over the entire United States, though it is really better at 5,000 feet or more. Do some shopping around to find the map you like best.

You're going to have to have a sectional if you're located near any control-tower areas. This is an FAA requirement and means you must know the rules of entering and leaving such a zone. In most control-tower areas, you can call the tower to say you'll be popping by and ask if it will be okay. Many of them prefer you to have a radio so they can spot you and warn other air traffic.

Rural areas are easier to fly in, as they enjoy a change in the traffic and may let you through without a radio. But you may want to carry a radio anyway, particularly if you're out for a record attempt or are in a competition. You can talk with your ground crew this way, and sometimes they can be a source of useful information.

Finally, the FAA requires you to know how to make out a flight plan, which simply means preparing a rough estimate of where you expect to be at a given time. Since the wind will blow freely regardless of your plans, you merely plot out the area in which you are probably going to be flying. You don't know for sure whether the winds at 3,000 feet will turn out as forecast, but you use them as basic data. You can always change your calculations if the forecast was wrong, though you may decide to come down if you're being blown toward a city.

Your flight-plan calculations will also include the time it takes you to ascend to your cruise altitude and the forecast wind's direction and velocity. You rough it out on your chart, write it down on a piece of paper, and then see whether it all checks out. If it doesn't, you correct and update, decide where you'll eventually be landing, and see if that checks out. You can play this game until you've used up two thirds of your fuel—then you should start looking in earnest for a place to land!

A Few Thoughts About Radios

*R*adios are rarely used in balloons, except during competitions or at particular events where other aircraft may be flying. There's still a possibility that you'll want to consider having a radio in your balloon for listening to weather reports or contacting your ground crew.

Since there's no energy supply from an engine in a balloon, you are limited to a battery or solar power source for your radio. The simplest way of dealing with this particular problem is to use a special aviation radio that contains its own battery. (You can, of course, take a regular battery and use those radios that have emergency adapters. You could also use solar energy panels if you have an "in" with NASA.)

Radios using different frequency transmit intelligence either as dots and dashes, on certain transmissions, or as voices using regular speech. Aircraft radios mostly use voice.

The various frequencies used for radio transmissions are chosen to facilitate communication. Assigned by the FCC (Federal Communications Commission), the bandwidths have been narrowed over the past five years or so and now revisions for 25 k/c spacing between frequencies are ongoing. From the point of view of balloonists, however, the information given below should suffice, since, as mentioned earlier, hardly any aeronauts make use of radio on a day-to-day basis.

Air Navigation Aids use frequencies from 108.1 to 111.9 MHz and 108.2 to 111.8 MHz—odd and even frequencies—and also 112.0 to 117.9 MHz.

The most important voice frequency is the international emergency channel on 121.5 MHz. This is a frequency you should remember at all times—121.5. A constant watch is kept on this frequency, and this is the channel you select when you have to call a Mayday (from the French, *m'aidez*—help me) should you be unfortunate enough to get into trouble.

The other frequencies are as follows:

118.0–121.4 MHz	Air Traffic Control
121.5 MHz	International emergency frequency
121.6–121.9 MHz	Airport ground control
121.95 MHz	Flight test—flying school
122.0 MHz	FSS en-route weather service ("Flight Watch")
122.05–122.15 MHz	FSS simplex or receive only with VOR
122.2 MHz	Available at all FSS for en-route service
122.25–122.45 MHz	FSS simplex
122.5 MHz	Tower: transmit and receive
122.55–122.75 MHz	FSS simplex
122.8 MHz	Unicom at airports with no tower or FSS
122.85 and 122.95 MHz	Unicom channels available for private airports
122.9 MHz	Multicom (agricultural, ranching, forest-fire fighting, parachute jumping) and air-to-air communication
123.0 MHz	Unicom at airports with tower of FSS
123.05 MHz	Unicom at heliports
123.1 MHz	Search-and-rescue and temporary tower
123.125–123.575 MHz	(25 k/c spacing) Flight test
123.30 and 123.50 MHz	Flying schools
123.6 and 123.65 MHz	Air Traffic Control
123.7–123.8 MHz	Air Traffic Control
128.85–132.0 MHz	Aeronautical en route (ARINC)
132.05–132.95 MHz	Air Traffic Control

You don't have to learn these frequencies. I've only included them for handy reference should you ever want to know them.

When using the radio, it is a good practice to keep your story short and sweet. The cardinal rule is to listen before you start speaking, wait until there's a moment of silence, then press the mike button down and speak. Unlike CB (Citizen's Band) radio, where the procedure is to call into a frequency to announce you are waiting to speak, aviation (and marine) radio has a stiffer etiquette. You really must wait until there's a silent moment before speaking.

This may seem very obvious, but all too many pilots—and some airline pilots, too—never bother to master radio technique. The problems arise when two people transmit on the same frequency at once. You get an electronic squeal that effectively cuts into the amount and quality of speech transmitted. So before chiming in, make sure no one else is there. If someone comes in fractionally after you, the tower—if that is whom you're calling—will recognize you provided you've got your identification in.

What may happen is something like this. In a regular airplane you'd be listening in on frequency (the control tower, that is) for your last forty or fifty miles before landing, so that you already have the local field data— i.e. the runways in use, the altimeter setting and any other special information. About ten or fifteen miles out, depending on your speed, you call to announce you are going to be arriving soon: "Teterboro, this is Cessna 20425 Uniform, Caldwell-Wright, inbound for landing." Then some other pilot comes barging in after you've started speaking, and the tower only gets the first or last part of your message. The tower will then say, "That Cessna, say again." Or, "Aircraft reporting at Caldwell-Wright, say again." You then repeat your message.

Unless you press the mike button down before you speak, you are going to clip the first words you say. The reason for this is that there is a slight time lag in warm-up of the transmitter. Keep the mike close to your mouth so you don't have to talk so loud that transmission is distorted.

In order to use a radio legally, you have to pay the government money. Unlike other countries, where all operators of radios are required to take an examination to show they know how to use the equipment, the FCC only requires two documents, plus a fee.

The first document is a restricted radio-telephone operator's permit. This is obtained by filling out the appropriate application form (753–A and B) and sending it with a check for eight dollars to the nearest FCC field office or to the main office at Gettysburg, Pennsylvania 17325. This permit does not allow you to make transmitter adjustments that may affect the proper tuning of the station. For that you need a first- or second-class radio-telegraph or radio-telephone license.

The second item necessary is a radio station license. With a transceiver aboard, your gondola is treated as a mobile radio station, and this document should be aboard at all times when the transmitter is being used.

Before applying for the license, check out Part 87 of the FCC Rules Governing Aviation Services (RGAS). Part 87 together with Parts 89, 91 and 93 can be found in Volume V of the RGAS. If you want to purchase a copy for permanent reference, the price at the time of writing was $12.50 for domestic subscription (including U.S. territories, Canada and Mexico). Money order or check should be made payable to the Superintendent of Documents. Required for application for the radio station license is Form 404 plus $20. Renewals must be filed for within thirty to ninety days prior to the expiration of the license. Actually, this is a tax on people who use radios, and works out to four dollars a year, as the license is good for five years.

These rules may be revised, so double check for the latest data.

A word about radio aids for pilots is appropriate at this point, since the FAA written examination usually includes a question or two about navigational beacons. While aeronauts have hardly any use for such devices, you are nevertheless encouraged as a good pilot to be familiar with what's going on elsewhere.

These radio beacons are navigational devices, and they work by transmitting data which are converted into information in the cockpit for the pilot. The most common, these days, is the VOR (Very High Frequency Omnirange) which transmits information telling the pilot what his magnetic bearing to the transmitter is, via a dial in his cockpit. If he places the needle in the center of the dial and keeps it there, he will fly to the station.

This is all very well in a powered aircraft, but not much use—save academic—in a balloon. The wind couldn't care less about radio beacons, other than flowing over and around them as it goes on its way.

The other type of navigational transmitter is the nondirectional beacon. A special radio called an automatic direction finder (ADF) has a compass card which shows the aircraft's course. A needle is free to rotate around the card, and when the frequency of the beacon is tuned into the radio, the needle points to that station, showing the direction in which the station lies relative to the aircraft.

Both VORs and ADFs are used for making instrument approaches, but hopefully, you won't be doing those in a balloon.

Radios make excellent sense for aeronauts making long-distance attempts. Malcolm Forbes, whose transatlantic bid was foiled by mechanical failure, had a most sophisticated system arranged for the record attempt. It involved the use of RCA's New York systems center and used satellite for constant voice contact throughout the flight from California to Europe.

Other aeronauts who have attempted transatlantic flight might be alive today had they taken advantage of radio communication. So radios do have a place in a balloonist's life, if not a very important one.

PART IV:

*Ballooning:
Past—
Present—
Future*

A Little Matter
of History

"The aerostat was so lavishly decorated that
one must suppose M. Montgolfier desired
that none should miss his new invention.
And indeed they did not—except, of course,
for all the animals and birds who, being in
their natural and unadorned state, flew in
terror at the sight of this many-colored
monster."

Gentleman's Magazine, 1783

*T*here is a great deal of evidence to show that the ancient
Chinese were familiar with flight—from rather sophisticated vehicles to
such primitive forms of ascension as ballooning. One story tells of an early
aeronaut—a woman by the name of T'a Ki, and a court favorite of a Yin
dynasty king, Chou-Hsin (1155–1121 B.C.) who for a wager prepared a
balloonlike vehicle and made a short but successful ascension.

The Indian *Mahabharata*—that national epic of more than 80,000
couplets which scholars believe to have originated as early as 7016 B.C.—
is very specific, and indicates the existence of an early, highly advanced
technology. It seems likely that these ancient peoples were also familiar
with the simpler forms of aerial transportation. There are several references
to construction techniques and even materials we have yet to rediscover.

Flying on the wings of the wind, as we know it today, was restored
to our consciousness quite recently; actually it coincided with the American
Revolution and demise of the French monarchy at the end of the eighteenth
century. Benjamin Franklin, ambassador to France, favorably influenced
the early American government in ideas of aviation. His interests in flight
were oriented toward the political and military significance of aviation, and

Test flying the Montgolfier balloon.

his thoughts on the subject remain well documented to this day. Franklin's main recommendation was that if some means were found for directional steering of balloons, the United States should form an air force regiment using these aircraft.

He was in France for the dawning of modern aviation, which happened something like this:

A pair of brothers called Montgolfier had a paper factory, and it occurred to them that they either had to diversify their operation, or advertise. Making a balloon had been discussed for a while, since they are excellent vehicles for advertisements. At that time, the balloon business was a totally new field of endeavor, and they thought some money might be made in building balloons. Furthermore, the research involved in developing a suitable mix for the paper (low flammability, etc.), could produce spin-offs that would benefit their paper business. Therefore, in the year 1783 the Montgolfiers were running a number of tests designed to minimize the dangers of combustion of the balloon fabric and reduce the chances of fire through sparks rising.

Another idea concerning flight was exciting the city of Paris at the same time. Designed by Jacques Alexander Cesar Charles, this was a hydrogen balloon, which used varnished silk for its envelope. The terms *Charlier* and *Montgolfier* are still used by afficionados today to describe gas balloons and hot-air balloons respectively. While the Montgolfiers were running their series of tests prior to their first manned flight, curiosity and excitement were building to fever pitch in the capital. Think back for a moment to the lunar expeditions in our own time and the excitement they generated, and you will understand some of the wonder experienced at the possibility of the first manned balloon flight.

Apparently alchemists of a speculative nature, the Montgolfiers thought that essence of fire caused the balloon to rise—that the smoke itself contained the lifting agent, which they named phlogiston, from the Greek word *phlogistos*, meaning fiery or flaming. In order to have an abundance of smoke, they burned damp stable straw and even old shoes. The stench from the smoke tended to discourage the nobility from assuming supervision of the project.

By June 5, 1783, the Montgolfiers biggest project to date became airborne. Benjamin Franklin reported that the balloon weighed almost 1,600 pounds, had a lift of nearly 600 pounds, and rose to a height of 6,000 feet over the village of Annonay, south of Lyons. The balloon was approximately ten meters in diameter and a little over twelve meters tall (about 30 $\times$ 38 feet).

The news of the Montgolfiers' success stirred the aristocratic French court party into action. A public subscription was raised to provide funds for the successful construction of a rival Charlier-type balloon. The first Charlier was successfully launched on August 27, 1783, and rose to 3,000 feet before disappearing into the low cloud cover. It landed about fifteen miles away and was immediately attacked by a group of farmers, who thought it was a monster from outer space and went at it with pitchforks. When it deflated, they tied the spent envelope to a horse and galloped it around to make sure it was dead.

Franklin was very impressed by the Charlier launch and devoted much of his time and energy to making balloons navigable. An attack of

First flight of the gas-type or Charlier aerostat, December 1, 1783, in Paris.

Captive aerostats employed on army maneuvers in Napoleonic times.

gout kept him in bed for the first hot-air balloon ascent from Versailles in September 1783, in which a sheep, a duck and a cock were sent aloft. The first thing everyone had to find out was whether it was possible for people to live in the air above. The flight was a success, and the stage was ready for a successful manned ascension of the *globe aerostatique*, as the hot-air balloon was called in those days.

The first tethered flight by man was made the following month, on October 15, 1783, when Pilâtre de Rozier rose to almost 100 feet. The first free flight took place on November 21. Rozier and M. Girond de Villette made a tethered ascent to 3,000 feet, and then Rozier was joined by the Marquis d'Arlandes for the first free flight from the garden of the royal palace in the Bois de Boulogne.

The French court party was still not satisfied at having made flight its national contribution, so a manned flight by a hydrogen balloon was arranged at the end of the year. J. A. C. Charles and M. N. Robert (who, with his wife, Anne-Jean, manufactured the rubberized silk balloon) went aloft on December 1, 1783.

Considerable experimentation was taking place in Britain, too, and a number of miniature hot-air and hydrogen aerostats were sent aloft during 1783 and 1784. It wasn't until August of 1784 that the first manned hot-air flight was made, by James Tyther in Edinburgh. In September, an Italian named Vincenzo Lunardi flew a hydrogen balloon from London to Standon in Hertfordshire.

The first American balloonist was Dr. John Jeffries of Boston, who went to England after the American Revolution to study medicine. Here he was propositioned by a traveling French balloonist, Jean-Pierre Blanchard, who needed some front money to cross the English Channel. John Jeffries agreed to pay—provided he got to go for the ride. The flight, which was not without adventure, took place on January 7, 1785, starting from Dover Castle. So much gas was lost through leaks that they bundled almost everything overboard, including Jean-Pierre Blanchard's trousers. They finally settled in the Forest of Guines, where John Jeffries grabbed a treetop to finish the flight. The world's first airmail letter was carried on this flight, from none other than William Franklin (the royalist son of Ben) to Benjamin Franklin's own grandson and secretary, William Temple Franklin. Thomas Jefferson, another of the Founding Fathers, was on hand to greet the pair.

The world's first flying corps was organized by Napoleon, under the direction of Andre-Jacques Garnerin, who made the world's first parachute jump from a balloon in 1797. It was Garnerin who arranged to publicize Napoleon's coronation by balloon, an attempt which was to backfire. Nine days after the coronation, on the evening of December 11, 1804, the coronation balloon, decorated with colored lights and embellished with the good news in gilt lettering, arose from the Place Notre Dame. It finally landed in Lake Bracciano near Rome, having snagged Nero's tomb on its way. Much wit was devoted to the fact that Nero had done Napoleon in. Garnerin was fired, and a woman aeronaut took his place. She was the wife of Jean-Pierre Blanchard.

The first woman balloonist was a popular operatic singer, a Madame Thible, who made an ascent at Lyons on June 14, 1784, in a hot-air balloon, *La Gustave*, with a painter friend, Monsieur Fleurant. According to this story, she arose belting out a song: "Oh, To Travel in the Clouds!"

The first English woman balloonist was a Ms. Letitia Sage, who wrote a pamphlet about her adventure. She flew with Vincenzo Lunardi and

*Ms. Letitia Sage made her aeronautical debut as the first English woman
aeronaut on June 29, 1785, and scandalized contemporary society with
her "shocking adventure." At left, British aeronaut George Biggin. The
famous Vincenzo Lunardi is at right.*

George Biggin from Newington Butts in northeast London to a field near Harrow School in the west.

And it was Jean-Pierre Blanchard who made the first balloon trip in the United States. His flight began in Philadelphia, which at the time was the capital of the nation. He was welcomed by General George Washington, and posted flyers announcing his flight to begin on January 9, 1793, promptly at 10:00 A.M. The local paper reported the next day:

> Mr. Blanchard, the bold Aeronaut, agreeably to his advertisement, at five minutes past ten o'clock rose with a balloon from the Prison Court (Walnut Street) of this city . . .
>
> The process of inflation was commenced at about nine o'clock. Several cannon were fired from dawn until the moment of elevation . . .
>
> When it began to rise, the majestical sight was truly awful and interesting, and the slow movement of the band added solemnity to the scene.

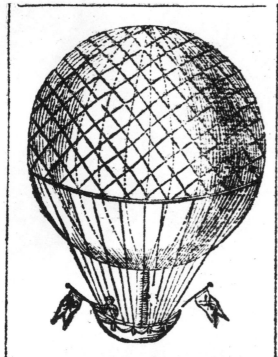

M. Blanchard's
FORTY-FIFTH AERIAL FLIGHT
Is positively fixed for Wednesday, January 9th, in the Prison Court, at 10 in the morning precisely, weather permitting.

———

Those who have subscribed on the blank subscription cards distributed thro' the city, are requested to end them to Oeller's Hotel, and those who wish to subscribe, may apply at the same place, until the 3d of January inclusively. Price of subscription, Five Dollars.

December 26.   mw&fif

First flight in America was undertaken by Jean-Pierre Blanchard, a French pioneer in aerostation. His flight lasted some forty minutes, and the crowds were grateful for the punctuality of the liftoff.

Aerostation was quick to catch public appeal and scenes were incorporated into the designs of fabrics, furnishings and pottery. Scene depicted here is from one of Blanchard's early flights.

Blanchard flew at about 5,000 feet and landed at Woodbury, New Jersey, some fifteen miles away. The locals for some time refused to come near the still partially inflated balloon. Blanchard coaxed them out of their fright by showing the passport he had from General Washington and plying them with liquor. It was his only American flight, as he didn't have enough money to bring equipment for more than one.

Some interesting developments in ballooning were carried out in England by Count Francesco Zambeccari, an Italian entrepreneur who sought asylum in London from the Spanish Inquisition. In early November 1783, he tested some unmanned miniature hot-air balloons, and in December he made a flight in a thirty-four-foot-diameter hydrogen balloon that supported a beautifully painted boat. His passenger was Admiral Sir Edward Vernon. An early liberated woman, an attractive Miss Grist, was ejected "with gentle force." He explained that she was only an accidental passenger, having climbed aboard for the thrill. Zambeccari wrote a book about ballooning, called *The Travels of Count Zambeccari*. He had many adventures and attempted to apply the principles of jet propulsion to steering balloons by using a pressure-lamp device which produced a jet of flame.

In June 1784, a year after the Blanchard ascent, a Baltimore lawyer, Peter Carnes, sponsored a couple of ascents, and—according to a report in the *Maryland Journal & Baltimore Advertiser*—a tethered ascent was made by thirteen-year-old Edward Warren, who volunteered to go up in Carnes's thirty-six-foot-diameter hot-air balloon. In July 1784, an interested crowd of some 25,000 persons, who had gathered for the public hanging of a pair of muggers, went on to watch the first free ascent by Peter Carnes himself.

As he took off, a gust of wind seized the gondola, dashed it against the prison wall, and out tumbled Carnes. The immediate loss in weight sent the balloon skyward to the cheers of the crowd—who still thought Carnes was aboard. At about 1,500 feet the envelope began to glow like a meteor and plummetted to earth, to the crowd's fascination. It was not until the following day that people learned of Carnes's narrow escape.

Americans were not very interested in ballooning at first, and several Europeans who visited the United States with hopes of turning people on to the sport couldn't even meet their expenses. By 1825 word had gotten around that Americans were skinflints when it came to ballooning; they would watch, but would not part with money. Bearing this in mind, Eugene Robertson, another Frenchman, demanded a minimum subscription of $1,200 before making the first balloon ascension from New York City. It seems that then, just as now, New Yorkers were willing to take greater risks than their fellow Americans.

Present at the ascension, which took place on July 9, 1825, from Castle Garden at the tip of Manhattan Island, was none other than the Marquis de Lafayette. He was making his first visit to America in more than fifty years, and a special celebration was being held in his honor at Battery Park.

Seats cost twenty-five cents apiece, but for fifteen dollars tethered ascents were offered. There were no buyers. Robertson used a hydrogen balloon, twenty-one feet in diameter with a capacity of some 5,875 cubic feet. The hydrogen was developed on site by the method of water decomposition. At 7:00 P.M., the elderly Marquis ceremonially cut the rope, and Robertson lifted off, waving flags to the crowd.

The first American woman aeronaut was a Madame Johnson, who announced that she would accompany Robertson on another ascension from Castle Garden on October 18, 1825. The New York *Evening Post* reported:

> The balloon being well inflated, the gondola was attached and the lady Aeronaut made her appearance. She is about 35-years old and was dressed in a white satin gown, with a red spencer. She gave the word to let go, bade her friends farewell, waved her flags, and rose with great rapidity, amidst the shouts of the surrounding multitude.

A successful flight was made across the East River, and they landed in the Brooklyn marshes "without the least injury except getting wet," as Madame Johnson told it later.

Robertson's father and brother were both interested in ballooning, and his father—Etienne Gaspard Robertson—produced a delightful plan for a seventy-ton aerostat, the *Sacrum Minerva*. It was large enough to carry sixty souls on a transatlantic flight of several months' duration, but there wasn't enough money to finance the project, and it was never built. Robertson's brother Dimitri made the first ascent in Calcutta, India, in 1835.

Robertson's next achievement was an altitude record of 21,000 feet. He made ascensions in 1827 at New Orleans, before going to Havana, Cuba, where he introduced ballooning. His last flight was at Vera Cruz, Mexico, where he died in 1836 of yellow fever.

It was Robertson who provided instruction to Charles Ferson Durant, a young scientist who saw the balloon as a means for exploring the planet's upper atmosphere. Durant was the first American-born balloonist, and he became a legend in his own time.

At the time of his first ascent, Durant was a relative unknown, according to a report in the New York *Evening News* of September 10, 1830, which noted the event at Castle Garden and identified the balloonist merely as "a person named Durant." On this flight, Durant landed at South Amboy, New Jersey, where people treated him as a hero before sending him back aboard a ship bound for the city. Durant quickly became a celebrity and was approached by Solomon Andrews, a young man who wanted him to test a model airship which, Andrews claimed, would sail into the wind. Durant declined the offer and went on to make a large number of successful ascensions which stimulated American interest in ballooning.

Andrews, meanwhile, was determined to fly. It took him a long time to succeed, but by July 4, 1849, he was ready to reveal his airship to the public. (He had to, since he wanted to head off a rival inventor, one Rufus Porter, who had formed a stock company to create an airship line to California.) *Knickerbocker Magazine* reported that "thousands of dollars have been expended in the project," which was a huge framework some eighty feet long, twenty feet wide and ten feet high. During the Civil War, Andrews even attempted to interest Lincoln in his invention, but the government wasn't responsive, and Andrews's efforts were pigeonholed.

Finally, Andrews decided to finish the work. He employed a fail-safe system using three cylindrical bags of Irish linen, each eighty feet long and approximately thirteen feet in diameter. Inside them he put twenty-one smaller balloons and then laced the three large bags together. A small (twelve feet) platform hung beneath the balloons. This airship was called *Aereon* and performed well on its maiden flight. The small balloons leaked, however, and Andrews substituted cloth partitions to ensure even distribution of the gas.

Aereon was an interesting vehicle, dependent on gravity to make it work. A report in the New York *Herald* describes a flight on September 4, 1863:

> Andrews set Aereon off in a spiral course upwards, she going at a high rate of speed and describing circles in the air of more than one and a half miles in circumference. She made 20 revolutions before she entered the first strata of dense white clouds, about two miles high, scattering them in all directions.

Andrews took out a patent* for the balloon the following year and developed the vehicle still further. He tested a lemon-shaped balloon and found that it could, indeed, navigate against the wind.

Interestingly, a few years ago a consortium of New Jersey businessmen put together a full-sized airship which flew using a small motor. They were unable to interest any bankers in providing capital to build a cargo-hauling version, and the project—which in ecological terms is far more sensible than 747s, not to say almost infinitely less costly in terms of resources—was shelved indefinitely.

Another airship** that could be steered was designed by Charles F. Ritchel of Corry, Pennsylvania. His vehicle worked a bit like a bicycle. It was a twenty-five-foot cylindrical envelope supporting a framework in which the pilot was seated, and pedals directed the thrust line of a hand-driven propeller. A picture of Ritchel and his machine appeared on the front cover of *Harper's Weekly* on July 13, 1878.

---

* Readers interested in the Solomon Andrews patent will find it listed as Aerostat, Number 43,449 and dated July 5, 1864.
** Dirigibles are balloons which are steerable and which may be non-rigid, semi-rigid or rigid. Rigid dirigibles are usually called airships.

Professor John Wise, another Pennsylvanian, made his first balloon ascension in 1835. He initially became interested in ballooning in order to further his studies in meteorology. But meteorology was forgotten when he became a nineteenth-century entrepreneur, making more than 700 successful balloon flights over forty years. In the late 1830s he invented the rip panel. Wise disappeared during one ascent over Lake Michigan in the fall of 1879, leaving behind a string of record flights.

Wise's first balloon—which he built by following instructions in a newspaper article on how to put a balloon together and generate hydrogen —was called *The Meteor*. It drew paying crowds on its first outing and thus determined that Wise would become a barnstorming aeronaut.

Like many others, Wise attempted to arouse government interest in a balloon project, only this one would save lives. The idea was to use an aerial warship during the Mexican Revolution to bomb the fortress of San Juan de Ulua, which guarded the port of Veracruz. By putting the fortress out of action from the skies, the Army would be able to take Veracruz itself with a minimum loss of life.

The project called for a war balloon 100 feet in diameter, capable of carrying two tons of explosives with which to blast the Mexicans out of the bay. As Wise stated in his petition to the military: "With this aerial war-ship hanging a mile above the fort, supplied with a thousand percussioned bombshells, the Castle of Veracruz would be taken without the loss of a single life to our army, and at an expense that would be comparatively nothing to what it will be to take it by the common mode of attack." The army rejected Wise's proposal and did it their way—with considerable loss of life.

Wise's attempts at balloon-bursting were based on his theory that in a terminal descent, the throat would fold in on itself and permit the gondola and occupants to parachute down. He discovered this was so when a balloon accidentally burst on him at 13,000 feet. After descending successfully he resolved to find out whether it would work every time— and many paid to see him do it.

His more serious projects concerned meteorology—proving the flow of a jet stream across America from west to east—and a transatlantic attempt. On December 20, 1843, Wise petitioned Congress for a $15,000-appropriation to construct a 100-foot-diameter balloon with which to plot the upper air winds as a means of drifting from America to Europe.

Following an ascent from Bellefonte, Pennsylvania, a year earlier, he had noted in his logbook: "It is now beyond a doubt in my mind established that a current from west to east in the atmosphere is constantly in motion within the height of 12,000 feet above the ocean." He told Congress:

> It has been fully demonstrated that there exists in the atmosphere a constant current of wind, moving from west to east, with a velocity of more than 60 miles an hour. It is even now feasible to travel eastward with a velocity that will circumnavigate the globe in thirty to forty days . . . which would enable us to leave dispatches in Europe and China, and return by way of Oregon Territory to Washington City.

It was sixteen years before he was able to test his thesis. A wealthy man, Oscar A. Gager, put up the necessary cash, and the two men formed the Trans-Atlantic Balloon Company. The balloon for the test flight was named *The Atlantic* and was fifty feet in diameter. Beneath the envelope a large wicker basket was suspended, from which Wise would pilot the machine; below the basket, connected by a short ladder, was a lifeboat cradled in a canvas sling.

Wise was accompanied on the flight by Gager; John La Mountain, another well-known balloonist; and Mr. John Hyde, a reporter from the St. Louis *Republican*. In addition to provisions, there was also a mailbag from the United Express Company. A reporter for another St. Louis paper spotted the mail pouch as he inspected *The Atlantic*'s car and noted that they also carried:

> . . . nine hundred pounds of sand in bags, a large quantity of cold chicken, tongue, potted meats, sandwiches, etc., numerous dark-colored, long-necked vessels containing champagne, sherry, sparkling Catawba, claret, Madeira, brandy, and port, and a plentiful supply of overcoats, shawls, blankets and fur gloves, a couple or three carpetbags chocked full of what is called "a change"; a pail of iced lemonade and a bucket of water, a compass, barometer, thermometer, and chart, bundles of the principal St. Louis newspapers; cards of candidates for clerking in several of the Courts, tumblers, cups and knives and perhaps other articles which have escaped me. . . .

On July 1, 1859, all systems were go. As evening fell, *The Atlantic*, filled with coal gas from the St. Louis Gaslight Company, lifted off and quickly picked up a strong west wind which bore it across Illinois at a healthy fifty miles per hour. It reached equilibrium at 8,000 feet, and the crew had a bottle of champagne and some roast turkey as the city disappeared in a pall of smoke. The moon shone that night, and the balloon envelope was illuminated by an eerie phosphorescence.

Wise settled down for some sleep, leaving instructions to maintain altitude by dropping out ballast if necessary. La Mountain—no doubt wanting to share the glory—made the balloon ascend too quickly and coal gas poured out over Wise, who escaped when Gager rescued him.

All went well for a while. By the following afternoon they were over the waters of Lake Ontario and faced with a cold front. They began a descent, only to find violent surface winds that drove them across the lake at speeds of up to ninety miles per hour. The lifeboat and car bashed against the water. Wise cut the boat free, and the balloon scudded upward. By evening, Wise decided that enough was enough, and they finally landed near Henderson, New York, with but two pounds of ballast remaining— the traditional bottle of champagne. As they prepared to toast, Wise figured out the distance. They'd covered 1,120 miles in twenty hours—the longest and fastest balloon journey ever made up to that point in time, July 1, 1859.

The Civil War interfered with Wise's plans to make a bid at the transatlantic crossing. He again tried to interest the military in his ideas and only succeeded in designing a bullet-proof basket to house observers. He wanted to form a corps of balloonists, but Thaddeus Lowe, a contemporary, was selected instead. Lowe was able to put on a demonstration for Lincoln thanks to his friendship with Professor Joseph Henry of the Smithsonian, and the President's endorsement was sufficient to put him on active duty as a civilian aeronaut working with the Army.

By the time the Civil War was over in 1865, *The Atlantic* was too old and tired to be used for a flight to Europe. Wise had to look for other backers, and the newly founded tabloid *New York Daily Graphic* offered sponsorship. Its publishers, the Goddsell brothers, at first agreed to Wise's requests that he be permitted to take his time in putting together the equipment, and that the public be prohibited from entering the work area in the Brooklyn Navy Yard. But the paper's circulation fell, and the Goddsells began admitting the public at fifty cents a head. Next they sold advertising space on the balloon, and eventually they moved it from the Brooklyn Navy Yard to a fair site, where there was more room for the public to view the monster—which was designed to hold 400,000 cubic feet of hydrogen.

Despite the steady flow of cash, the Goddsells began pressing Wise for a quick launching. Wise protested that he wasn't ready, that there was a weakness in the crown that had to be fixed. The Goddsells weren't interested and replaced Wise with his assistant, Washington Harrison Donaldson, formerly an aeronaut with Barnum's Traveling Hippodrome.

The balloon was inflated and Donaldson was set to lift off when the fabric gave way, smothering the crowd with hydrogen. Wise left New York the same day. After numerous repairs, Donaldson finally got the balloon up, only to land forty-one miles away in New Canaan, Connecticut.

Wise wrote two books—*A System of Aeronautics*, which was a handbook for those interested in flight, and his autobiography, *Through the Air*, which was read by the Swedish engineer Salomon Andrée, who was planning a flight to the North Pole by balloon. The two were to meet at the Philadelphia Centennial World Exposition in 1876.

Before continuing with the American picture, let's see what was happening in Europe.

The most serious pioneer ballooning took place in England. Charles Green, son of a rich fruit vendor, received an education in the sciences and became interested in gases. Green reckoned that ballooning would be considerably cheaper using coal gas and became the first person to use the commercial gas as a lifting agent. He continued to use coal gas throughout his distinguished career.

Green's first flight was made in honor of the coronation of George IV in 1821. He rose to a height of 11,000 feet, and except for a rough landing, the flight went off perfectly.

During his more than thirty years of ballooning, Green never experienced a single accident, though he carried nearly 1,000 people as passengers or crew. He also owned and made a number of balloons, including the enormous *Royal Vauxhall*, which developed sufficient lift to carry eight passengers on its maiden flight from Vauxhall Gardens in London. It was in this same balloon that Green made his famous flight to Germany.

Robert Holland and Thomas Monck Mason were friends of Green's and both were captivated with flying. They were also rich. They offered to fund the expenses of inflation and provisions if Green would agree to pilot them for a long-distance attempt. After some consideration, Green said yes, and it was from the preflight planning of this trip that the drag line came into being.

The concept of the drag line was twofold. First, it was a means of adjusting ballast, since the more line that is overboard and resting on the ground, the less weight in the gondola. And secondly, the drag line could be used with a grapnel to slow down flight, rather like slinging an anchor from the sky. The proliferation of telephone and power company wires across the landscape has caused the demise of this aid.

The *Royal Vauxhall* was stocked with provisions for a two-week cruise, including forty pounds of cured meats, Bath Olivers (a famous English biscuit similar in flavor—though not in texture—to the graham cracker), several dozen bottles of good port, sherry, claret and brandy, and hundreds of pounds of sand for ballast. Without flight crew, the gondola weighed some 3,000 pounds including 2,000 feet of drag line, parachutes for dropping messages and a nonflammable quicklime stove for brewing tea.

The three adventurers set off from Vauxhall Gardens in the early afternoon of November 7, 1836. Their flight path initially took them toward Uxbridge, north and west of London, exactly the opposite direction they wanted. Green let the balloon ascend until he found the right air currents, and by three o'clock they were heading for the English Channel.

As the winter sun slid slowly down, they flew high over Dover Castle toward the white cliffs at a healthy twenty-five miles per hour. At 4:48 P.M. Mason recalled later, "the first line of waves breaking on the beach appeared beneath us, and we might be said to have fairly quitted the shore of our native soil, and entered upon the hitherto dreaded regions of the sea."[*]

The white cliffs melted into obscurity, and the loom of Dover lighthouse formed a marker for their course. By 6:00 P.M. they were over the French coast and moving along steadily at 3,000 feet. They feasted, and Mason described their first meal as follows:

> The bench was quickly spread with the good things that had been abundantly provided to cheer our solitary flight. Cold meats of various kinds, beef, ham, fowl, and tongues, together with bread and biscuits, and a mixture of wine and other liquors, formed the basis of a repast which might in truth have proved acceptable to much more fastidious palates than ours.

Then the flameless stove came into play. Green had invented this stove in order to heat things during flight. The principle was simple. When slaked with water, quicklime produces intense heat without a flame. The heating was done by attaching a kettle to the top of the stove and hanging the cooker and kettle over the side of the balloon for safety. It worked fine, and the water boiled promptly. Tea and coffee could be prepared.

Later that night they wanted to brew more tea, but the cooking device slipped and fell. This meant there was no further need for the lime, which could be dumped next time ballast was required. Since a barrel of lime

---

[*] Monck, Thomas Mason, "Account of the late Aeronautical expedition from London to Weilburg," London, 1836; *Aeronautics*, London, 1838.

could hurt a person, they decided to attach the barrel to a small parachute to moderate its descent.

It was a dark, moonless night, and soon the lights from the foundry plants at Liège were visible. As they floated closer to the ground, they could hear the sounds of voices. They brought the balloon further down, lighted a flare beneath the gondola, and started to call out in German and French to the workers.

By dawn they had ascended again to 12,000 feet and were so cold—their water had frozen—that Green was obliged to valve off some gas to get them down to warmer air. Below, all was snow covered, and the sun rose to reveal three chilly aeronauts who had no idea where they were.

When it was time to descend, there was a brisk wind, and it took some time to get the grapple to hook on the ground. As they got out of the gondola they noticed a few peasants watching them from behind some trees.

"*Wo sind wir?*" asked Monck Mason, the interpreter.

"In the Duchy of Nassau," was the reply. "But where are you from?"

"*Aus London, England.*"

There was much astonishment and congratulations, and no doubt some champagne, too. The three had flown nearly 500 miles since 3:00 P.M. the previous day, a seemingly impossible feat.

They were treated royally, and local honors were showered upon them. The trio became the subject of popular songs, and when finally they got back to England they were treated as heroes. Green changed the name of the balloon to *Nassau* to commemorate the event.

Green continued his ascensions until his retirement from flying in 1852. He was the first person to propose a transatlantic attempt, but was too old and therefore unable to go. He did make one other record—unintentionally, as it turned out. Robert Cocking, an elderly gentleman, wanted to test a new parachute he had designed and he persuaded Green to take him aloft. When Cocking went over the side, the balloon rose to an altitude record of 23,000 feet. Cocking and his equipment weighed 400 pounds and Green was prepared for the balloon's reaction, having fitted additional valves to vent off the gas. Cocking, it is sad to relate, like Icarus before him, fell to earth and died when his parachute failed.

By the 1850s ballooning had become so popular that airways were beginning to develop. Unfortunately, the farmers weren't very happy about this; they complained that balloonists were ripping up fences and trees with their grapples, as well as frightening their livestock. In Essex—an agricultural district to the north and east of London and a favorable spot for landing—the farmers organized to harass the aeronauts. They set traps in their fields, using spring guns and other injurious inventions to deter the adventurous. If they caught a balloonist, he was likely to end up before a kangaroo court, with a stiff fine, a night in jail, and a heavy settlement for alleged damages.

Into this milieu came a more modern type of aeronaut with more technical knowledge. Balloons were now carrying scientific equipment and even crude cameras to take aerial pictures of the earth's surface. Wise's ripping panel was used, considerably aiding aeronauts in landing. Enter Henry Coxwell (1819–1900) and James Glaisher (1809–1903), both of whom made remarkably high altitude ascents.

Coxwell quickly became a successful balloonist after a couple of flights from Vauxhall Gardens. He became professionally involved and even attempted to sell the German military his own war balloons. The Germans were impressed when he dropped bombs from his gondola, and agreed to purchase two vehicles from him.

James Glaisher was a research scientist at the Greenwich Observatory, where he headed the Department of Magnetics and Meteorology. He was familiar with balloon flight and thought it the best means for exploring the atmosphere. He sent a paper to the British Scientific Association setting forth his proposals for a series of high-altitude flights for research into the composition of the air. When the association agreed to the project, Glaisher persuaded Charles Green to come out of retirement for the flight.

While Green was fit for piloting, his balloon's envelope was not. There were two malfunctions on the ground before the material burst. After similar problems with other balloons, Glaisher approached Coxwell with the proposal that he make a special high-altitude research balloon.

By 1862 the balloon was ready, and Glaisher decided to go on its maiden voyage, even though he had never flown before. Project head-quarters was at Wolverhampton (about as far from the sea as you can get in England, to avoid a wet landing), and the local gas company supplied the coal gas for the 90,000-cubic-foot-capacity aerostat.

On their first flight, Glaisher and Coxwell went to 26,000 feet, on their second to 24,000 feet, and on their third—which was nearly their last—to an estimated 36,000 feet. At a height of 29,000 feet, Glaisher began losing consciousness. Coxwell was fixing a valve line which had become twisted, but returned to arouse Glaisher. The balloon continued ascending at 1,000 feet per minute. Coxwell, too, found himself becoming powerless. He grabbed the valve line with his teeth and dipped his head two or three times until the balloon started to descend. It is unlikely that anyone will ever again attempt their record ascent without oxygen or pressure suiting.

As a team, Glaisher and Coxwell made numerous ascensions, both by day and by night. Glaisher continued to fly, and his book *Travels in the Air* is a classic. He enjoyed flying so much that he founded the Royal Aeronautical Society. Coxwell also lived to a ripe old age and, during his twenty-seven years of ballooning, is believed to have made more than 1,000 ascents. During that time he experienced not a single accident, and he never failed to make a scheduled ascension.

In the United States, meanwhile, a Professor Carlincourt (whose real name was Thaddeus Sabieski Constantine Lowe) had become a rival to John Wise. In much the same way that small children today are interested in automobiles and airplanes, Lowe was fascinated by balloons.

With the help of John Wise's *A System of Aeronautics*, Lowe's first balloon, *Enterprise*, was a complete success. He was soon able to build sport balloons for a living, and in 1858 he made a successful ascension at Ottawa, Canada. To celebrate the completion of the first transatlantic submarine cable by Cyrus Field, Lowe began construction of a transatlantic balloon at Hoboken, New Jersey. It was named *City of New York* and was the biggest balloon at the time. With a capacity of 725,000 cubic feet of coal gas, the balloon envelope was 130 feet high with a diameter of 104 feet. More than 6,000 yards of cloth were used in its construction, and the gondola was twenty feet in circumference. Using coal gas, the balloon would have a lifting capacity of more than eleven tons. (With hydrogen, it would have exceeded twenty tons.)

The Manhattan Gas Works was unable to deliver the volume required, and Lowe was invited to move to Philadelphia, where he was sponsored by Dr. John C. Cresson, owner of the Point Breeze Gas Works. Lowe completed his machine there and renamed it *Great Western* at the suggestion of Horace Greeley. In the summer of 1860, a perfect test flight was made, and by September all was ready for the transatlantic attempt. The balloon was filled, but the weather was bad. The *Great Western* was caught by a heavy gust of wind and rapped against its mooring post, ripping the envelope. It would be at least a year before another transatlantic attempt could be made.

Meanwhile, Lowe decided to test out the wind system on a flight east to Philadelphia from Cincinnati. On April 19, 1861, Lowe lifted off in *Enterprise* and landed at Pea Ridge in South Carolina. The flight was a record. In just nine hours, Lowe had flown 900 miles, a record speed for the time. But the Civil War had just begun, and to Southerners, balloons meant Yankee spies coming in by air. Lowe and his balloon were hauled off to the local jail. Fortunately a local innkeeper recognized the balloonist and persuaded the rural militia to let him be responsible for Lowe until the authorities could be informed. A local official turned out to have been to college with Lowe and was able to arrange a safe-conduct.

It was undoubtedly the fact that Lowe had good military information in addition to his being a reputable balloonist that got him the job of organizing the Union's air corps. Lowe was helped by Secretary of the Treasury Salmon P. Chase, who invited him to Washington to personally present his plans to the President. But Lowe was also a good publicist. While waiting for an appointment to meet with Lincoln, he began making ascents and generating his own gas from the grounds of the Smithsonian Institution.

Lowe presented the novel scheme of installing a telegraph in his captive balloons so that information could immediately be given to command. Lincoln was impressed, and Lowe arranged for a demonstration using *Enterprise* with a telegraph operator. Lowe told the operator to transmit the following message to the President:

BALLOON ENTERPRISE, WASHINGTON D.C. JUNE 18, 1861.

TO THE PRESIDENT OF THE UNITED STATES:

SIR:

THIS POINT OF OBSERVATION COMMANDS AN AREA NEARLY FIFTY MILES IN DIAMETER. THE CITY WITH ITS GIRDLE OF ENCAMPMENTS PRESENTS A SUPERB SCENE. I HAVE THE PLEASURE IN SENDING YOU THIS FIRST DESPATCH EVER TELEGRAPHED FROM AN AERIAL STATION AND IN ACKNOWLEDGING INDEBTEDNESS FOR YOUR ENCOURAGEMENT FOR THE OPPORTUNITY OF DEMONSTRATING THE AVAILABILITY OF THE SCIENCE OF AERONAUTICS IN THE SERVICE OF THIS COUNTRY.

T. S. C. LOWE.

When Lowe finally came down, a note of congratulations was waiting for him from the President. Lincoln also approved his request for materials, labor and money, and a Union air corps was in the making. As is usual in such projects, there was plenty of indifference from the government bureaucracy and the military. Officials got in Lowe's way; officers wanted manpower, not balloons. As he began to get the corps underway, Lowe was ordered to the front. As Wise had done, he had to fill *Enterprise* from the city gas supply and tow the balloon to the front.

There was considerable fear that Confederate troops might be gathering together for a mass attack in late July 1861. From his position on a tether, Lowe could not find any evidence of this, but accurate intelligence would require a free flight into Confederate territory—and the winds to bring him back.

Finally, he was given permission, and he went deep behind the Confederate lines near Fairfax, Virginia. His observations showed that the fears of an attack were nonsensical. But no winds appeared to bring him home. It was almost dark when Lowe made his landing, and no one noticed. He rolled the envelope up and settled down to sleep. Lowe was considerably surprised to be awakened first by a column of Confederate troops, and later by four men who stated they were Union troops and had come to find him.

"How in hell did you find me here?" asked Lowe. Then the men told him that his wife—who worried about him on all his flights—had plotted his approximate course and suggested a likely landing place. The men told Lowe they would get a wagon for the balloon and return him to Union territory. At dawn a woman leading a team of mules hauling a wagon came out of the mist. It was Lowe's wife, Leontine. She told him to stow the envelope in the back, cover it with hay, and hide underneath. Mrs. Lowe then drove them back to Arlington, Virginia, and Lowe went off to report to the generals. The officials were so relieved by the optimistic news and Lowe's successful return that he now received the cooperation he sought.

Lowe's corps of balloonists did well for the Union troops, and he played an important part in the defeat of the South by providing intelligence by telegraph to General McClellan's Army of the Potomac—from the balloon gondola to the general's office, as he had demonstrated to Lincoln. His balloon corps was responsible for developing a signaling system that enabled the artillery to send their lethal cargoes with greater accuracy. The result threatened balloonists, since the Confederates were quick to realize the danger of the "eyes in the sky." Lowe's field gas generator, which worked by pouring sulphuric acid over scrap iron in a zinc-lined container, worked sufficiently well to be used on an aircraft carrier during the Civil War. This was another first. Lowe was a success.

Interested observers from other nations came to watch these proceedings. They included a British captain, George Beaumont, who would later form a balloon corps for the British Army, and Count Ferdinand von Zeppelin, who bombed London nearly half a century later with his dirigibles.

But army life did not agree with Lowe. He contracted malaria, and with his retirement from the front, balloon activity began to dwindle. The Southerners formed a balloon corps of their own, but their efforts were minor and never really followed through.

Professor Thaddeus S. Lowe seen here observing the Battle of Fair Oaks, Va., May 31, 1862. Lowe popularized usage of military observation balloons, updating them to include signaling equipment.

While recovering from malaria, Lowe invented a process for artificial refrigeration and patented a process for making artificial gas. He became quite rich and retired to Pasadena, California, where he founded the Pasadena Gas Works.

Lowe is also of interest for performing the first marriage ceremony aboard a balloon at Mount Vernon, New York. He became interested in astronomy and built an observatory at Mount Lowe in California. Lowe also devised the process of producing acetylene gas for lighting and welding. Unfortunately, Lowe died before *Lowe's Planet Airship*—a superballoon expected to outperform the Zeppelin airships—was completed, and the possibility of his being first to circle our world in a balloon was gone.

Sketch of balloon boat Washington *and its captive aerostat—from Civil War period.*

Above left: Signals Corps balloon seen here at Tampa, Florida, in 1898.

Above right: War balloon being deployed at Santiago, Cuba, in 1898.

Right: More modern version of Signals Corps balloon, here at Fort Myer, Va., in 1908.

It was the Civil War which finally convinced the military of the effectiveness of balloons at war. The proposal was originally filed by an army colonel named John H. Shelburne back in 1840. But it took a Presidential directive to get the military to move on the subject more than twenty years later.

Since that time, balloons, blimps and dirigibles have been used by the armed services with varying degrees of success. The U.S. Army had a balloon in Cuba which was used on June 30, 1898 by aeronaut Ivy Baldwin to confirm rumors that Admiral Cervera's fleet lay at anchor in the harbor of Santiago de Cuba during the Spanish-American War. The U.S. Signal Corps also made use of balloons in campaigns against the American Indians.

More recently, observation balloons were used extensively during World War I when 100 U.S. balloons were shot down in action. They were also used for both defense and attack purposes during World War II.

Balloons are still being used for propaganda purposes. The Goodyear Tire and Rubber Company, which produced more than 1,000 balloons and some 100 non-rigid airships during World War I, is still in the business of building airships. Today four of these are used for public service and public relations, and may be seen at major football games and other events where an aerial TV platform comes in handy.

Each airship carries sophisticated night signs on either side using color and animation which can be read from a mile away when flying at 1,000 feet. Goodyear has followed a corporate good-neighbor policy with regard to this type of advertising for several years, and some 75 percent of all night messages must be of a public service nature. These days energy conservation reminders and gas-saving tips vie with such worthy causes as The Heart Fund, American Cancer Society and dozens of others. (Interestingly, the blimp will operate eight hours a day for nearly a week on the amount of fuel it takes a big jet to taxi from the ramp to the takeoff runway.)

While military usage of balloons will undoubtedly continue, since for observation purposes they are unique, more and more people are discovering that balloons offer far more opportunities for pleasure, self-discovery and science. Hopefully, the days when they were used for sneak attacks on other human beings are gone forever.

Airships:
Dirigibles
and Blimps

*T*he word *dirigible* doesn't mean "risibility" or plastic. It is derived from a Latin verb meaning "to steer" and was originally used to describe balloons that could be steered directionally. It has come to mean the cigar-shaped motor-driven type vehicle with a cabin or car slung beneath the main structure, and is frequently used to describe the rigid airship.

Actually, there are three varieties of airships. The non-rigid (like the Goodyear blimp), the most common type, is usually small (comparatively speaking) and keeps its shape from the pressure inside. The only reinforcement can be found at the nose and tail.

The semi-rigid has a keellike structure running along its underbelly, a trelliswork of high tensile girders, light in weight but immensely strong. This helps maintain the shape, along with the actual pressure of the gas inside.

One might wonder if this could present problems in flight, since changes in temperature, pouring rain, and atmospheric pressure—not to mention load factor—all affect a dirigible's equilibrium. In order to prevent the gas bags from bursting or taking on a soggy sausage shape, some form of adjustment is needed.

This is done by fitting additional air bags inside which maintain proper envelope pressure and additionally serve to trim the dirigible's attitude.* It is for this purpose that blimps and semi-rigids have an airscoop in the propeller slipstream: it feeds air into these auxiliary bags in the envelope. As far as the airship pilot is concerned, bag pressure is the primary concern aboard, and a device called a manometer—somewhat similar to the equip-

---

* Attitude describes an aircraft's position relative to the horizon. It refers to where the nose is pointed and includes the degree of bank in a turn.

First successful American airship was US Army dirigible No. 1, built by Thomas Scott Baldwin—a veteran parachutist and aeronaut—seen here undergoing trials near Fort Myer in the summer of 1908. Previous airships were less successful, though Dixon's airship is worth a comment—Cromwell Dixon was a teenager whose mother helped him put his ship together.

*Italian M–1 the forerunner of an extensive line of medium-sized dirigibles developed
during WWI. Capacity was around 440,000 cu.ft. and the car was suspended to a sectional hinged-type keel that ran fore to aft by means of parabolic wires sewn into the
envelope between each keel joint. A forward gun platform was later positioned above
the bows.*
Vital statistics: 265 feet. Width: 59 feet. Engines: 2 x Itala 280 h.p. Gross lift: 13 tons approximately. Cruise: 40+ mph.

*R 23 was designed and constructed by Vickers Ltd. of Britain and put into commission
as a training ship in 1916. She is seen here about to release a small airplane. The hull,
made of duralumin lattice girders, contained 18 gas compartments for a total cubic
capacity of some 942,000 cu.ft. when full. A gun platform can be seen above the bows
and was reached by a climbing shaft passing between gas bags two and three.*
Vital statistics: Length: 535 feet. Diameter: 53 feet. Gross lift: 23.6 tons. Useful load: 5.8 tons.
Engines: 4 x Rolls-Royce 250 h.p. with the fore and aft engines driving a pair of swivelling 4-
bladed props. The two engines in the center gondola drove non-swivelling single props. Maximum speed was 55 mph, with a cruise of 40+ mph. Duration was 50 hours only.

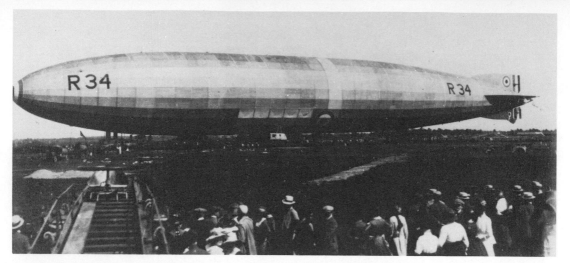

R 34 was the second of a modified rigid class (R 33) airship based on data obtained and prepared by the British Admiralty from the wreck of Zeppelin L 33, shot down over Britain in 1916. She was completed in 1919 and is seen here on arrival at Lakehurst, N.J., July 6, 1919. She was the first LTA to make a successful double Atlantic crossing. Basic data: Along the bottom of her hull is a keel corridor formed of A-shaped girder frames, which provided the crew with a means of moving from one gondola to another, in addition to housing fuel, stores, water ballast and bombs and ammunition. A forward gun platform was provided on top, near the bows, and an after gun pit was situated behind the top fin. Interestingly, R 34 had a wireless aboard, and the radio operator's "office" was in the forward gondola. There were 19 gas chambers for a cubic capacity of 1.95 million cu.ft.

Vital statistics: Length: 643 ft. Diameter: 78.75 ft. Gross lift: 59.2 tons. Useful load: 30 tons. Engines: 5 x 250 h.p. Sunbeam "Maori," two of which were fitted with reversible props. Maximum speed was 65 m.p.h. with a cruise of 45+ mph.

Seen here is a DN–1 US Navy dirigible, an early "blimp," very similar in design to the B and C class Submarine Scout-type airship developed by the British Naval Air Service. Designed for coastal patrol work, she had a capacity of around 180,000 cu.ft. and a crew of up to four people. Noteworthy is the double dorsal fin and the band encircling the lower portion—a drip flap to prevent rain and condensation from falling on the crew. The tube leading like an umbilical cord from the car to the bottom of the envelope is to provide air to the balloonets and maintain envelope pressure. Cruise around 50 mph.

DN–1 seen here about to leave her floating hangar. The year is 1917.

ment which measures your blood pressure—is used to measure the pressure inside the envelope. The air bags—or balloonets, as they are more properly called—are fitted fore and aft, and by filling and emptying them in coordination with the elevator, fairly exact up-and-down control is provided.

The third variety of dirigible is the rigid or great rigid, which, as its name implies, is made of a complex latticework of intricately placed light metal within which walkways (catwalks), stowage areas and even crew quarters are provided. The lifting gas is stowed in numerous bags within this framework along with additional space in which to expand (or contract). Should the airship reach an altitude at which there is a danger of bursting, a special emergency venting system permits gas to be valved off.

Directional movement is provided by thrust from the propellers: up-and-down movement and left-and-right steering comes from an elevator/rudder section at the stern. Cables are moved forward from these control surfaces to the pilot's station from which the airship is directed. The impression—even in a blimp, which is a mere babe compared to the monsters of former years—is not unlike steering a large ocean-going ship, since a certain amount of anticipation is required, and the vessel itself rides the invisible waves of the skies.

An engine failure, unlike in fixed or rotary wing aircraft, is no big deal. If, for any reason, the engine or engines should stop, the airship behaves like a regular balloon. It is for this reason that airship pilots also receive balloon pilot training. The basic difference between flying an airship and flying a balloon is that an airship is a balloon which can take you some-where you want to get to, whereas a balloon will take you where the wind blows. However, modern airplane pilots should be warned that it is by no means as easy as it sounds!

While an airship is a bit more like an airplane than a balloon—since on takeoff and landing it must be kept head to wind—the speeds and angles of attack involved are likely to give conventional pilots a bit of a challenge. There is also a need for ground assistance and guy ropes from the nose area together with stern wires and lines from the control car.

As with balloons, a buoyancy test must be conducted on airships and blimps before lift-off. Each big ship has its EQ (equilibrium quotient) which is when the vessel rides free, neither sinking nor climbing. The parameters are quite generous, and the bigger Goodyear blimps are per-mitted to take off and land up to 800 pounds heavy. But weighing off, as it is called, must be done prior to takeoff and landing.

In passing it might be noted that while the manometer is the number one instrument in semi- and non-rigid airships, the gas temperature gauge runs a close second, and is the most important instrument in rigid airships. The altimeter is the instrument of next importance.

Finally, everything's in order and the skipper calls out "Let go!" or "Up ship!" The engines are firewalled (as conventional pilots would say) and very soon the ship has become airborne. Depending on conditions, dynamic lift—where airspeed is used to move the ship up—may be used. Steep climb angles are the norm and cruise altitude—usually around 3,000 feet—is reached shortly. For landing the procedure is similar in that buoyancy must be tested and the airship brought carefully into wind. You do not crab a dirigible into a landing—you land exactly into the wind's eye. Depending on how heavy the ship is, the landing crew may take bags of lead shot aboard to make sure you've finished flying, once you're down.

In the old days hydrogen gas was used in all British, French, German and Italian airships despite the fire hazard. American airships used helium, and with today's surplus of helium (wholesale price was 12.5 cents per cubic foot in mid-1976) everyone uses it. The Goodyear blimp—which contains more than 200,000 cubic feet of helium—is thus flying around on more than $25,000 of the stuff. Leakage is normally around about 1 percent or less per month.

The term "blimp" has puzzled many, but most agree that it was a contraction of a military designation of a World War I British airship known as "Balloon Type B, limp." Unfortunately, this widely accepted epithet turns out to be so much hot air, according to Dr. A. D. Topping, editor and historian of The Lighter-Than-Air Society.

Topping, who scotches another theory that "blimp" is a contraction of "bloody limp"—claimed by some etymologists to stem from the British habit of lacing their language with adjectival "bloodies"—says that credit must go to Lieutenant (and later Air Commodore) A. D. Cunningham of the Royal Naval Air Service, who, in December 1915, was commanding officer of the British airship station at Capel.* On Sunday, December 5, 1915, Cunningham was conducting his weekly inspection of the station and stopped off at a hangar housing an SS–12** airship. During his inspection Cunningham playfully flipped his thumb at the gasbag and was rewarded with an odd noise from the fabric.

Smiling, he flipped his thumb again, and then imitated the sound: "Blimp!" The midshipman commanding the SS–12 repeated the tale to

---

* See correspondence columns of British magazine *The Aeroplane*, July thru November, 1951.
** SS = Submarine Scout.

*River barrage balloon units played an important role in
the defense of London during World War II.*

fellow officers before lunch the same day. Thus the origin of the term
blimp; it has come to mean non-rigid or semi-rigid balloons which may
or may not be dirigible. The barrage balloons which defended London and
other cities during World War II, and which were used by the allied navies
to defend convoys against the Luftwaffe and—in the case of the seaborne
balloons—against submarine attack, were non-dirigible blimps. The Goodyear blimps—*America, Mayflower, Columbia* and *Europe*—are all dirigibles.

The first blimps, you could say, were the tethered balloons (fore-
runners of the famous Kite Observation balloons) used by the French
military at Maubeuge in 1794. Parachute landings were first carried out
some three years later from this type of equipment by A. J. Garnerin in
Paris. And Jean Baptiste Meusnier, Napoleon's Air General, designed a
system which, if it worked, would have been the first true dirigible. Shaped
like a futuristic egg, the system called for a streamlined gondola slung
below in which ninety men would provide the muscle to turn a propeller
and drive it forward.

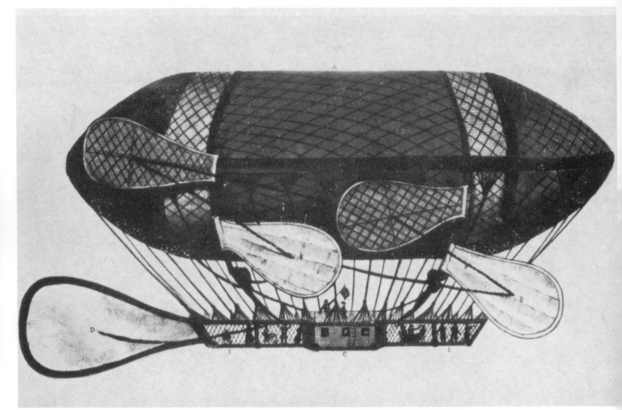

Some designers were not as well equipped as was Sir George Cayley in understanding the concept of thrust as applied to the air. An early dirigible design—Lennox's Aeriel Ship the Eagle *shows a primitive paddle system to drive the craft along.*

But many difficulties were uncovered and a full-scale model was never tested. It was not until 1837 that the first true dirigible was designed by the father of western aviation, Sir George Cayley, the Yorkshire baronet. In 1799, at the age of twenty-six, Sir George had designed the first true airplane, based on the separation of the concepts of lift and thrust. Later he put his theories into practice, and modern aviation owes him a great deal. Interestingly, the Cayley dirigible design is somewhat like the lighter-than-air craft flying one hundred years later in the 1930s. A streamlined gas bag gave lift to the vehicle, and propulsion derived from a steam engine connected to propellers. A rudimentary rudder device provided directional control with a simple elevator to move the vessel up and down. Unfortunately, though many admired Cayley's design, no one was prepared to put up the cash to produce a prototype.

In 1850, Pierre Julian, a Frenchman, designed a clockwork-powered model dirigible. This so inspired compatriot Henri Giffard that he put the whole thing together in a full-scale version. This vehicle proved capable of making the seventeen-mile journey from Paris to the hamlet of Trappe at a good six miles per hour—not very fast, but better than walking. It was 140 feet long, 40 feet in diameter, and had a weight problem, with the 3.5-horsepower steam motor weighing nearly 400 pounds. Giffard, an experienced railroad engineer, was more than a merely competent balloonist. He recognized the limitations of his vehicle and suggested something more than ten times as long to cope with the weight of the engines. His search for a light, more efficient means of propulsion led to the use of electricity as a power source.

Giffard's giant balloon with Arc du Caroussel at right.

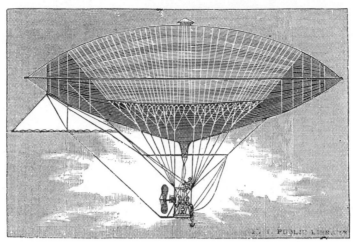

The brothers Albert and Gaston Tissandier's airship.

There were a number of electric dirigibles in the late nineteenth century. The best known is the product of the Tissandier brothers. In 1882 the brothers Albert and Gaston Tissandier installed eighteen batteries and a 1.5-horsepower motor in their ninety-two-foot-long airship, attached a propeller and sailed gently away at three miles per hour. The following year, the French government funded a similar successful project suggested by two officers.

It was not until the internal combustion engine came along that the dirigible really arrived. The engine, in the form of a Daimler Benz motor, did not lead to immediate success, however, as there was still much to be learned about the use of hydrogen as a lifting gas.

In 1897, David Schwartz's unique aluminum-covered balloon, with a number of individual gas cells inside, blew up on its maiden flight. The gas had expanded on lift-off, swelling the individual cells far beyond their original capacity—a possibility which had not been considered. The resulting pressure slit open the seams of the exterior.

Some years earlier, Count Ferdinand von Zeppelin of Germany had been thinking about getting into the dirigible business himself. Three years of research with an engineer named Paul Kolber resulted in plans which were presented to Kaiser Wilhelm II, a virtual dictator who wanted to prove himself a brilliant general.

Zeppelin, it will be remembered, had visited the United States during the Civil War and was intrigued with the balloon corps' efforts. He'd made an ascension at Fort Snelling, Minnesota, and was sufficiently interested to develop his airships for postal usage and travel. A military capability was important, too, if government funding was to be obtained, and Zeppelin's pitch was that his airships would be immensely successful for naval reconnaissance.

Luftschiff Zeppelin *No. 1* was some 420 feet long and took off from its floating hangar on Lake Constance on the German border on July 2, 1900. The first of a series of flights, this testing proved her to be structurally sound, although the steering systems were still rather rudimentary. She was severely damaged on reentering her hangar.

It took another nine years for the worst snags to be ironed out of dirigible construction and for Zeppelins to lead the world in this type of aircraft. But the public fancy caught on early, and national pride—and a desire to outshine the French, who were then leading in heavier-than-air craft—soon produced government money. A newspaper report from these

The LZ–4, basically similar to the –3 series, was forerunner of a long line of airships generally reckoned to have been the best in the world. Count Ferdinand von Zeppelin had been a cavalry general in the German Army and had visited the US as a young officer to observe military activities during the Civil War. He made an ascension in a captive balloon at Minneapolis during his stay. Passed over for promotion, he decided to build airships. Three years of research with a civil engineer named Paul Kolber produced plans that were submitted to the Kaiser and the German military, who were not impressed. His first airship, completed in 1900, was damaged on re-entering its floating hangar, and he was able to solicit private funding to build a second. The military were still not interested, and it wasn't until public opinion was aroused that government funding became available. A passenger service was soon established, and by about 1910 the word Zeppelin *had become currency in the western world for any rigid airship.*

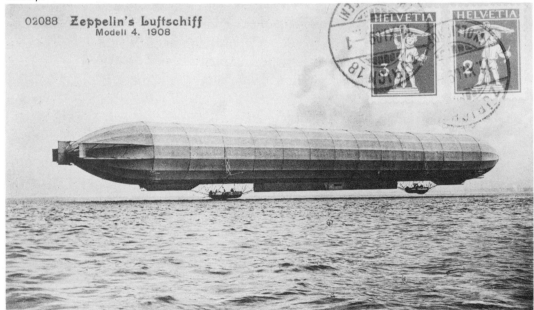

02088 **Zeppelin's Luftschiff**
Modell 4. 1908

early days indicates that the German government felt the possession of such aerial warships would give them a sizable advantage over the more conventionally equipped British.

By the time World War I broke out, the Zeppelin's potential ceiling of approximately 22,000 feet, which would keep it out of the range of conventional fighters, was being planned. Its cruise speed would be nearly eighty miles per hour by the end of the war, and it would have a duration of more than a week for a still-air range of some 11,000 miles. During the war, its lifting capacity was to be increased to sixty tons, and bomb loads of 2.5 tons per ship were being carried.

At the same time that Zeppelin's first dirigible was getting underway, a South American millionaire playboy, Alberto Santos-Dumont, came to Europe and thrilled the Parisian café scene with his extravagant lifestyle. He made his first balloon ascension in 1895, which set the pattern for a fervent interest in flight in France. He took time out from his automobile racing to try to win the 100,000-franc prize offered by French oil billionaire Henry Deutsch de la Meurthe for a flight from St. Cloud to the Eiffel Tower and back in thirty minutes, a distance of seven miles.

He designed a series of dirigibles, each a little bigger and a little faster than the one before. By October 1901, Santos-Dumont had completed *Number Six* and was ready for the attempt. He woke the press corps and Deutsch de la Meurthe from their beds and made a night attempt. A wind delayed them for twelve hours. When it was calm, Santos-Dumont got into his machine, started the engine and took off. He sped off over the roofs of Paris at about 800 feet, straight for the Eiffel Tower. Then the drag line got caught on a rooftop, almost ripping the gondola from its gasbag. He cut it free and went on. It took just six minutes to reach the Tower and as he circled round for his return, Dumont waved a hand to the crowd below. Homeward bound, the wind blew up again, forcing him to use full throttle against it. The ignition system, not designed for such treatment, started to break down, and its faltering led to explosions in the exhaust system producing sparks out of the tube. Dumont switched the ignition off. He then secured the control wheel and walked forward to adjust the ignition timing. Meanwhile, the *Number Six* had been drifting backward, almost touching the Eiffel Tower.

Dumont finally got the motor started again and slowly revved it to full throttle. It was going to be nip and tuck that he'd make it. Everyone was looking at their watches. Deutsch de la Meurthe was dancing with impatience; no one knew for sure whether he was pleased or not. The officials' stopwatches ticked off the seconds running out to the half-hour.

Alberto Santos-Dumont, a Brazilian by birth but raised and educated in France, built some 16 airships from 1898 on. In 1901 he won a 100,000 franc prize donated by oil magnate Deutsch de la Meurthe for his Eiffel Tower race. Here is a real life portrait and a caricature from the time.

Here's how Dumont described it:

On the trip back I kept my eyes on the greenery in the Bois du Boulogne, and used that as a sort of cross bearing on the reflective silver streak of the Seine at the point I had to cross.

I was in there at around 450-ft, throttle to the firewall as I was flying over Longchamps, and then across the Seine, keeping on with the power over the heads of the Commission and the spectators at the Aero Club.

It was exactly eleven minutes and thirty seconds past three o'clock, for a time of precisely twenty-nine minutes and thirty-one seconds for the flight.

Good enough to win, right?

Our momentum carried us well over the finishing line, and I turned and descended for them to catch the guide line, and I yelled: Did I win? and the people below yelled back and screamed that I had.

Dumont shared the 100,000-franc ($30,000) prize with his crew and some of the poor of Paris. The Brazilian Government Encouragement Prize of $20,000, which he also won, went—according to a report in the *Times*— "on its specific objects of Paris experiment and local Brazilian exhibitions. In truth," continued the article, "Santos has spent several fortunes from his own great revenues in these experiments."

You might call the stunt good public relations.

Dumont made himself one of the top men in Europe through his money and his genuine skill. He was a born charmer and was easily accepted as a working-class hero by the Parisians, who admired his dash, his skill as a mechanic and the fact that he was generous with his prize money. After showing what could be done with ordinary balloons, Santos-Dumont turned his efforts to regular airplanes, which were just becoming popular.

He financed a "People's Plane" called the *Demoiselle* which was to sell for $1,000. It was the least expensive airplane on the market, and only the people manufacturing it made any money. But people didn't speak kindly of the *Demoiselle*. They felt it was an excellent, practical flying machine, but apparently one had to be something of an acrobat to fly it safely!

With Dumont blazing the trail for a successful marriage of gasbags and engines, Zeppelin quickly built up public enthusiasm for his type of dirigible. His airships were large and rather luxurious.

Count Zeppelin had already proven that his dirigibles could provide effective transportation. (The German Airship Transportation Company* began regular scheduled passenger service as early as 1910.) Two dirigibles had fallen into the hands of the Allies. One, a raider caught in France, was carefully copied and after the war resulted in the building of America's first rigid dirigible, the *Shenandoah*.

Built in 1919, the *Shenandoah* made a number of successful early flights from east to west, but a storm in 1925 cracked the hull in three places.

Lt. Commander Charles Rosendahl was in the forward section, which had sufficient buoyancy to climb away from the scene, and without any engines, he piloted the craft safely back to earth using his experience as a regular aeronaut.

The *Akron* and the *Macon*—both American-built craft—were also both beaten down by the weather. These two airships had a number of interesting design innovations, such as water-recovery systems, internally mounted engines, and the capability of housing, launching and retrieving small fighters.

---

* Dr. Hugo Eckener, perhaps one of the finest airship pilots in history, joined Count Zeppelin in 1909, and was directly responsible for the development of the world's first passenger air service. On March 4, 1912, the small Zeppelin *Victoria Louise* carried 23 passengers some 200 miles in eight hours. By the end of 1913, more than 400 journeys had been made. And by August of 1914, when World War I broke out, *Victoria Louise* with sister ships *Sachsen* and *Hansa* had covered between them 65,000 miles and carried more than 19,000 passengers. The airship factory produced twenty-four Zeppelins between 1900 and the outbreak of war.

Framework of USS Shenandoah *during construction and in flight over the Hudson River.* Model number ZR–1 Shenandoah *was a Zeppelin copy, but unlike the German-built product her structure failed during a good-will tour in September 1925. Her forward section was piloted back to earth as a free balloon by Lt. Comm. Charles Rosendahl, saving some of her crew.*

Cabin of the passenger-carrying Bodensee Zeppelin offers equivalent comfort to jumbo jet first-class seating today—and that was in 1910. The seats even swivel around for a better view.

The Los Angeles, a German-built LZ–126 seen here landing on USS Saratoga during fleet exercises in January 1928. Of the US Navy's airships, she led a charmed life from the time of her arrival in 1924 until she was decommissioned in 1932.

USS Macon, *sister ship to the ill-fated* Akron, *which crashed in a storm off the Jersey coast on April 3, 1933, seen here during flight maneuvers, July 7, 1933. The small aircraft hovering like pilot fish beneath this aerial whale are F9C–2s and are about to hook on. Inset shows docking mechanism. In 1935 the Macon's upper fin collapsed in turbulence and she sank off the California coast after control had been lost. Two crew members died—they panicked and jumped too soon.*

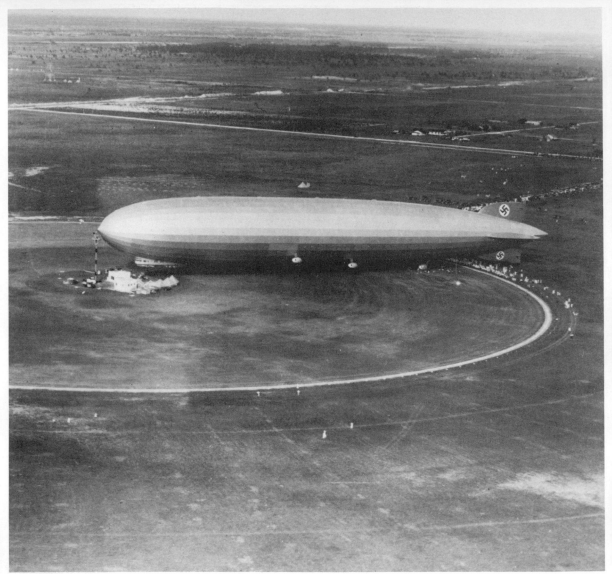

Graf Zeppelin *seen here at her moorings. Note swastika rondel on upper and lower tail fins. These beautiful airships were swiftly adopted as a public relations tool for Hitler's brand of corporate fascism. ITT, Dow Chemical, Texaco, were among many American corporations indirectly supporting Germany's bid for world domination.*

Insert shows restaurant aboard, where gourmet-style meals were regular fare. Completed in 1928, Graf Zeppelin was the predecessor of the ill-fated Hindenburg. *During her years of service she visited the North Pole, the Pyramids, and worked a regular passenger- and mail-carrying service between Brazil and Europe. Fitted with five engines of 530-hp, she cruised at more than 80-mph.*

The Hindenburg, *last word in modern airship design, seen here at her mooring mast, Lakehurst, N.J., May 20, 1936. Because of a US government embargo on sales of helium to Nazi Germany, she used hydrogen for lift and was equipped with innumerable safety devices perfected after more than forty years' experience with this flammable gas . . .*

. . . yet she exploded just a year later, May 4, 1937, while coming into her mooring mast in America. Sabotage? Or accident?

The fourth big naval airship was a German-built LZ–126 acquired by the United States after the war by way of reparations. Renamed *Los Angeles*, she was flown transatlantic in the fall of 1924 and served without accident until decommissioned in 1932. It seems quite extraordinary now that the German-built airship—until the *Hindenburg* disaster, which took place over American territory—should have enjoyed such an excellent service record, whereas none of the other airships did. And what induced the British to use the R–101 instead of the R–100 (a much better vessel in every respect) is another of those questions which historians may reveal answers in future times.

Dirigibles went out of favor with the crash of the *Hindenburg*, which could have been the ultimate airship of our time. It was more than 800 feet long with an internal capacity of better than 7,000,000 cubic feet—the growth from the wartime versions, which barely made 2,000,000 cubic feet, was considerable.

The power supply had been increased a great deal, with four 1,100-horsepower Mercedes-Benz diesels pushing her along. Cruise speed was just short of eighty miles per hour, and passenger accommodations were deluxe. Only seventy passengers could be carried aboard, and for those who could afford the $400 needed to cross the Atlantic in two days, it was an experience not to be missed. It was the first night-coach air service in history. The pressure-pattern flight plans meant an average flight time across America of sixty-five hours eastbound and fifty-two hours westbound.

Once you got into the *Hindenburg*, the accommodations were clearly superior. Each stateroom was provided with two berths like a deluxe motel room, with hot and cold running water, showers, expensive comfortable beds, fine linen and personalized room service with stewards. An electric kitchen—the *Hindenburg* used hydrogen, because we embargoed our helium—and distinguished kitchen staff provided 300 gourmet-style meals per day, accompanied by fine European wines. Deck accommodations included a spacious lounge and bar area, a reading room complete with up-to-date periodicals and magazines, plus a small library. A wide gallery and promenade deck ran on either side of the sleeping quarters. All the furnishings and other objects aboard were specially designed to be light-weight, right down to the chess sets. Both the bar and smoking room were pressurized as a safety factor, and strict no-smoking rules applied elsewhere. The lounge featured an aluminum piano and a large plate-glass window through which you could look almost directly down.

During the first year, ten successful round-trip flights were made. Then, curiously, disaster struck on the first trip of 1937, as the airship was coming into dock at the Lakehurst, New Jersey, naval station. Two hypotheses offered at the time suggest either static electricity or a backfiring diesel (!) as the cause of the explosion. The Los Angeles *Times* reported:

CAUSE OF BLAST MYSTERY

What caused the fateful blast just at the moment the great craft was being moored, no one knew. The explosion occurred at the rear and some observers believed a spark of static electricity following a mooring rope from the ground set off the highly inflammable hydrogen. Other reports indicated a backfiring motor might have sent a flash of flame into a minute gas leak.

However, it is highly unlikely that with the throttles back and the engines running sweetly at low revolutions, anything like a backfire would occur through the spark-proof muffler systems.* Sabotage is a more likely answer, and Michael M. Mooney in his book *The Hindenburg* suggests some possible reasons why this may be so. Certainly the inquiry never produced any evidence, but we've seen so many tragedies in our time where law-enforcement agencies have committed and covered up crimes that this would hardly be anything new.

The *Hindenburg*, filled with helium, would certainly be a much sounder and more ecologically desirable machine than many of the aircraft which have come after her. True, we can now cross the Atlantic in six and one-half hours, but we also consume an enormously vast quantity of fuel. Since the oil industry controlled the helium, and aircraft like the *Hindenburg* threatened oil sales, the oil companies are more than likely to have had an interest in the development of fuel-intensive equipment.

Certainly dirigibles would make an enjoyable way of traveling around the world in great comfort. In a time of vast unemployment, they would be considerably more labor-intensive vehicles than the average 747, which requires a great deal of equipment to run, though not too many people. The *Hindenburg* crew-to-passenger ratio was 6:7, which must also have made for an enjoyable flight.

The U.S. military, however, went along with the blimps, as soft-cover dirigibles are called. As captive balloons, blimps were highly successful during World War II in providing protection—first against the German bombers, and later against the V–1 flying bombs. They were often used

---

* New York *Daily News* editor Duke Krantz stated that the engines were stopped prior to the series of explosions which ripped through the airship.

D-Day, June 6, 1944, when the Allied armada landed in occupied France.
Barrage balloons provided protection from an already wounded German
Luftwaffe.

Barrage balloons provided aeriel protection as LSTs unload at Nisida,
Italy, August 9, 1944.

Goodyear blimp America. *The dots on the side are lamps that provide computer-controlled advertising.*

in groups from which were suspended wire cables that were virtually invisible in the air.

Blimps could also be successfully used for observation purposes, even at sea. But they were slow and could not compete with fixed-wing transportation. As low-level observation platforms, blimps seem very useful, and they can also weather strong winds.

Raven Industries, more than any other corporation, has made ballooning a recognized popular sport once more, and in 1974 produced a new hot-air blimp, the *Starship Enterprise.* The "star" part of the name stands for Small Thermal Airship by Raven. The *Enterprise* is 120 feet long and 48 feet in diameter, with a volume of 140,000 cubic feet. Fully loaded (with fuel and crew of two), *Enterprise* has a gross load of 2,100 pounds and a three-hour endurance.

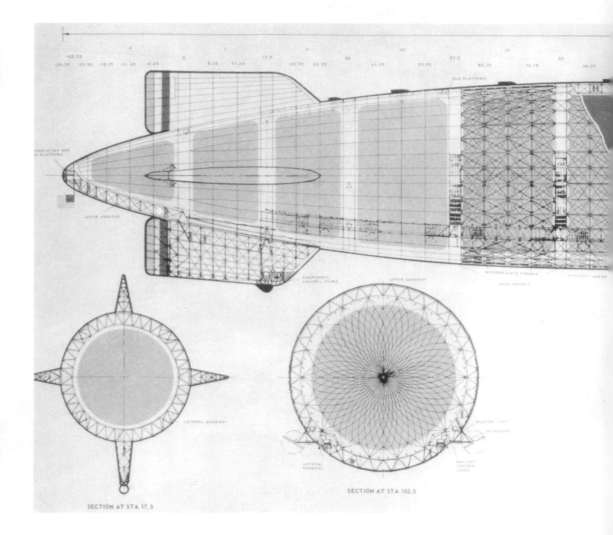

SECTION AT STA 17.5

SECTION AT STA 102.5

Compared with the Goodyear Blimp *Columbia*, Jim Winker, the Raven project's test pilot, says the Goodyear ship is the Cadillac of the two. The *Columbia* has a cruise speed of nearly fifty miles per hour, while *Starship Enterprise* moves at only about twenty to twenty-five miles per hour. Power sources differ, of course. *Columbia* sports a couple of 210 Continental engines, while *Enterprise* makes do with a much modified Revmaster VW aero engine.

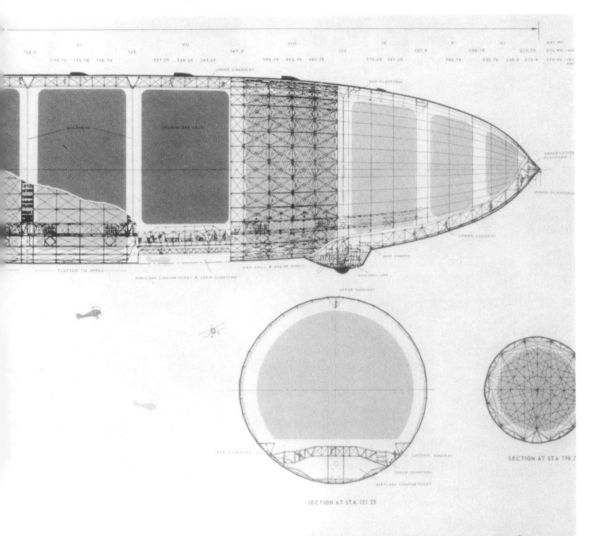

The incredibly complicated latticework of girders required for airship construction is vividly demonstrated in this sectional plan.

Besides its use in advertising, the Raven blimp looks as though it may sell for environmental work, traffic observation, oil-spill warnings and the like. While not as handy as a helicopter in terms of covering the ground, the initial price is much cheaper, and the maintenance and fuel costs are considerably less expensive. Estimates place *Starship Enterprise* at under $40,000 to produce, and that's cheap compared to a regular blimp, which can run up to $500,000.

High Flyers

"Ye People of America, ye wise and happy
Nation, who knowing the full value of liberty—and not insensible to that of a just
submission to the laws—you attracted all
my attention, and the desire of beholding
you in the full enjoyment of the blessings of
liberty, under the protection of your newly
established government, find my soul as
much as the wish of acquiring some glory
among you . . ."
J. P. Blanchard
First Ascension in America
1793

*B*allooning today is very definitely a pursuit of the adventurous person. To join the club, you have to be unpuckered about
hanging over the side of a fragile basket suspended beneath a piece of
fabric filled with either gas or air and dear Mother Earth drifting downward
and away from you.

If you are seriously interested in aerostation, it's courteous to know
something about the many heroes of the art. In our time, there's Ed (Paul
E.) Yost, generally considered the father of modern hot-air ballooning,
and a person who probably holds more patents in the field than anyone
else on earth.

Another name to know is Jimmie Craig, a former associate of Yost's
and U.S. National Hot-Air Balloon Champion in 1964 and 1965. Craig
is one of the most experienced pilots in this sector of aviation with nearly
1,000 hours logged in hot-air and gas balloons. And there's the Piccard
family, who have enjoyed a position of leadership and innovation through
three generations. Of the newcomers, look to Tracy Barnes, who seems
likely to revolutionize aerostation with solar-energy balloons.

As you get into ballooning, you'll discover other, equally well-known souls. Where ballooning differs from most other forms of human endeavor is that while records are set eagerly, there's always the understated acknowledgment that humans are merely mortal and can only try to live like gods and move through the skies.

When a record gets set, everyone is relieved as well as happy that odds have been taken and won. So far, no one has been able to make a successful transatlantic crossing in a balloon, though many have tried.

The earliest real distance event was undertaken by Charles Green with Robert Holland and Thomas Monck Mason from London to the Duchy of Nassau in Germany. The distance was 480 miles in about eighteen hours, on November 7–8, 1836.

John Wise set a record in his *Atlantic* on July 1, 1859, with his flight to Henderson, New York, from St. Louis, a journey of nearly 1,200 miles in twenty hours.

In 1857, while Felix Nader was taking aerial pictures of Paris from balloons, other aeronauts were crossing the Alps—which is still a popular ride, as the strong wind currents are well known. He was one of the guiding lights of the aeronautical movement which enabled Paris to survive the siege of September 1870 with an airlift by manned balloons.

Nader's *Guide for Aeronauts*, an eight-page pamphlet for amateur pilots, still contains useful material. There are notes about navigating and the importance of bodies of water for checkpoints. Interestingly, Nader and his colleagues used long streamers of paper to indicate whether a balloon was in equilibrium, rising up or doing down. He also stressed the importance of remaining calm, especially once a descent has begun, and the need for care in dropping moderate amounts of ballast over the side. Nader suggests it is always preferable to wait for a spontaneous descent of a gas balloon, which at the end of a day will come down as night moves in, cooling the air. If valving of gas is required, careful attention must be paid to the two coordinates of the approach path—that of the vertical and horizontal descent.

While the politicians were busy reshaping Europe, scientific endeavor was moving along slowly. No balloons had been to the poles of the earth, but they seemed to offer a sporting chance of getting through the bitter cold.

In 1893, Salomon August Andrée, a Swedish engineer who had studied with John Wise some seventeen years earlier, received a grant that enabled him to make his first balloon, *Sweden*. His flight planning was so good that on its maiden flight *Sweden* was able to climb to more than 13,000 feet and stay aloft for nearly three hours. His second flight lasted seven hours, and his third saw him blown across the Ahvenanmaa Straits to Finland, a distance of 170 miles in ten hours. During this flight, he experimented with rope dragging for steering and was sufficiently encouraged to work out a system which would provide a reasonable degree of steerage. The basis of the system was a steering sail which could be moved around in respect to the relative wind, plus a three-part drag line that trailed along the ground. Apparently this system produced directional deviation of up to 30 degrees from the normal ground track.

Andrée prepared a carefully documented brief pointing out that given an aerostat that could be steered and the prevailing south to north winds over northern Norway during the summer months, a balloon flight to the North Pole was a reasonable possibility. The balloon for the job would have a double silk envelope with a cubic capacity of more than 210,000 cubic feet of hydrogen. He attached details of the sail steering system to be used, plus a proposed drag-line system. The lines would be made floatable by using coconut fiber. The gondola was ambitious, containing a darkroom and berths for three. Ancillary equipment included provisions for four months, sledges, a collapsible canvas boat, a tent, firearms and ammunition.

It was all carefully worked out, and the Swedish Anthropological and Geographical Society was invited to lend a helping hand in the funding. But while public and scientific interest was high, no one wanted to put up the money to erect the hangar for the balloon and its construction. Finally, dynamite magnate Alfred Nobel made a commitment, and the expedition was soon funded.

A Frenchman, Henri Lachambre—one of those who had flown out of Paris during the 1870 siege—was appointed to build the polar balloon *Eagle*. Dane Island, a small island off Spitsbergen, far north of the Arctic Circle, was chosen for the launch site. Here, in the summer of 1896, the balloon hangar was built. It was constructed to open right out at lift-off protecting the balloon from buffeting winds until it was airborne. A small, unmanned test balloon was used to check out the entire system, and it all worked perfectly. It was decided to go ahead with the inflation of *Eagle*, even though the northerly winds necessary to get to the North Pole had yet to blow.

They waited out the remainder of July and the entire month of August, and still the winds blew southerly. When the first snows announcing winter arrived, they had to call off the trip. Andrée's return to Stockholm was unpleasant; he was treated as something of a rip-off artist who had failed to perform. The following summer, when Andrée and his two crewmen—

Nils Strindberg and Knut Fraenkel—returned to Spitsbergen, there were a couple of critical paragraphs in the morning paper.

The balloon hangar had survived the winter very well. Nevertheless, the explorers kept a careful check on such matters as leakage and replaced the gas that escaped on a daily basis so the *Eagle* could make her getaway to the north as soon as the winds permitted.

Considerable attention was paid to the drag-line system, since this ballast (the lines were also being used as ballast) could produce effective altitude control below 3,000 feet AGL (Above Ground Level). In addition, the drag lines provided some degree of directional control when used in conjunction with the sail. A quick-release mechanism had been designed so that should a drag line catch foul in an ice crevice and hold the balloon, it could be released momentarily.

Finally, on July 10, 1897, two seal boats pulled into Dane's Island harbor for shelter from an incipient storm from the south, said the skippers. The explorers made last-minute preparations, and the following morning they noted that indeed the wind had shifted round, gusting up to a gale force northwards.

At 11:00 A.M., Andrée announced that the flight was on, and the *Eagle* would take off as soon as the hangar was open and all were aboard. There was a precious lull in the wind, and the order was given to cut away. Majestically the *Eagle* climbed.

But not for long. Passing out of the protection of the balloon hangar, a gust caught the aerostat, carrying the gondola against the topmost branches of the windbreak of trees. It almost sent Andrée spinning out to the ground. Crossing the harbor, the balloon was knocked down almost to the water, hitting the topmost waves. It rebounded upward as the crew dumped ballast to get altitude. The drag lines were also left behind. The fierce winds gave the balloon a twist and carried it up out of sight.

Three days later a carrier pigeon brought the first word in a message which read "Weather delightful. All well on board. In excellent spirits." The pigeon had been downed by a skilled shot from a Norwegian fishing vessel. And then there was a long silence. It was not until the summer of 1930 that a sealer arrived in White Island, far north of Spitzbergen, a popular stop for killing seals. It was here that the remains of the expedition was found. It was not cold and exposure that killed the men, but their eating polar bear which gave them trichinosis.

The story of this flight has been well documented. Without drag lines, it became almost impossible to steer the balloon; the flight had been planned to ascend a mere 600 feet AGL. By the second day, the *Eagle* had drifted some 250 miles to the north of its intended course. Later that day, freezing fog brought about condensation of the gas and ice on the exterior fabric of the balloon. By late afternoon the balloon was forced down to the ice. The remaining ballast was off-loaded and the *Eagle* went forward over the ice floes, occasionally flying, but mostly bumping.

Three days after starting out, Andrée pulled the rip panel. They rested until July 17 and then began to march south to the nearest of three supply camps that had been set up for just such an emergency. By the beginning of October, they set up camp on an ice floe drifting south. The portion of ice they were on broke and settled on White Island, where they set up their final camp. Some time after October 17, it all ended.

Despite the disappearance of Andrée's expedition, polar exploration and ballooning continued to thrive. Long-distance events became important social occasions, and one moved Count Henry de la Vaulx, a French banker, to make his debut in the long-distance stakes with a flight across the Mediterranean from Paris to Russia. The trip was nearly 1,200 miles and lasted thirty-five hours, which was not as good a record as John Wise's trip nearly fifty years earlier. The 400-mile flight to Algeria from Marseilles took a mere ten hours. The count continued his interest in aviation, became a power-plane pilot, and ended his career about thirty years later, when he collided with some power cables near Newark, New Jersey, and was electrocuted.

It was inevitable that government bureaucracy would get involved in ballooning. The French started it by issuing diplomas for pilots of free balloons—have a diploma and prove to your friends you can fly was the appeal. By 1913, the French Aero-Club had issued licenses to nearly 400 free balloonists.

Meanwhile, Walter Wellman had designed a dirigible, *America*, which would go to the North Pole. His report in the *Review of Reviews* in 1908 gives details of the craft:

> In designing our ship we followed the French type, maintaining the rigidity of the form by means of interior pressure, and balloonets. These balloonets are filled, when occasion requires, by a 5-h.p. motor, driving an air blower. This type enables us to get a machine of reasonable dimensions, getting a very high lifting force over the machine itself to be used for fuel for the engine, provisions, instrumentation and the necessary equipment required for long distance flight.

It is worth noting that in the early days, there was still considerable doubt about whether a crew would be able to survive the rigors of weather—especially the cold. While the distance from Spitzbergen to the Pole was only 700 statute miles, the conditions were hardly like a thruway.

Wellman continues: "I have always thought that there is great advantage in the French type of balloon after landing, because of the lesser surface presented to the force of the wind. A ship of the French type would enable us, on a storm coming up, to quickly deflate the gasbag, and the possible damage would be small."

Wellman's *America* was designed more for endurance than speed. A cruise range of 2,100 miles was established, so that at the end of the 1,400-mile round trip, there would still be fuel for an alternate. Cruise speed would be around twenty miles per hour for the trip, using an eighty-horsepower Antoinette eight-cylinder motor.

Wellman experienced many of the same setbacks that plagued Andrée. In 1906 he had to postpone the trip because of the lateness of the season for getting underway. In 1907 the vehicle encountered an arctic storm and was driven back. Wellman was undaunted, and in 1908 he made yet another attempt, which was fraught with mishap. First the main engine broke down. Next the guide rope parted, sending the dirigible into clouds 5,000 feet above the sea. It was decided to valve off gas, descend, and be taken in tow by the *Fram*, a ship that was exploring the northern waters at the time. The guide rope was being used to store provisions, and without enough food the expedition was definitely off. But fate had not finished with *America*. Just as it reached the landing stage to be lined ashore, a gust of wind caught the huge envelope, snatching it away from its mooring and carrying it over rough ice hummocks for a short distance before it exploded.

About this time, several women were taking to the skies. Katherine Wright and Mrs. Jack Van Deman both flew with Wilbur Wright during the early 1900s. Ruth Neely of Los Angeles seems to have been the first woman actually to pilot a dirigible in America, and she was a special attraction at the Aviation Week celebration in 1910. "Aerial Queen Will Hover Above City; Aviation Week to Be Graced by Woman Flier," read one headline.

Neely's airship was sixty feet long and seventeen feet wide. The pilot sat over a gas tank which contained enough fuel for eight hours of flight, while at the stern was a system of rudder and elevators with which to direct the machine.

According to a summary of the year's activities, the highest ascension made by manned balloons in 1909 was by two Italian aeronauts, Messrs. Piacenza and Mina, in their *Albatross*. On August 9, from Turin, they ascended to 30,350 feet. A footnote indicates that a record of 34,450 feet was set by Berson and Suring on July 31, 1900.

The greatest height attained by an unmanned balloon (balloon-sonde) was recorded by the Uccle Observatory in Belgium on November 5, 1908, at 29,040 meters (eighteen miles).

The first people to make political statements using aerostats were the English suffragettes. In 1908 Muriel Matters, noted for her militancy in the women's liberation movement of the day, ascended in a soft dirigible on behalf of the Women's Freedom League. Her aerostat bore the simple legend: Votes for Women.

Meanwhile, Lincoln Beachy was making his debut as a dirigible pilot at the First in America Aviation Meet. A report in the May 1909 issue of *Cosmopolitan* magazine portrays the last word in aviation costumes for women, and pictures two of the women who were flying. One was the Baroness de la Roche, a pilot from France, another was Madame O'Berg, who flew as the guest of Wilbur Wright. The baroness was something of a daredevil, having raced cars and motor launches successfully. Her career as a pilot was cut short when she panicked during an aviation meet at Rheims, France, in July 1910, and became an early victim of the stall-spin syndrome in her Voisin machine. It was not her first accident, but she died in it. It was from a similar aircraft that the Russian flying ace Captain Macievich was thrown out, having set an altitude record at St. Petersburg (now Leningrad) of 3,633 feet on October 7, 1910.

Just a week later, the indefatigable Walter Wellman set out from Atlantic City, New Jersey, for Europe, in another dirigible named *America*. Larger than his polar machine, this dirigible had a cigar-shaped gasbag 228 feet long and 52 feet wide, and a lifting capability in excess of twelve tons. It supported a steel car which contained gas tanks plus three gas-powered engines. The main engine, eighty horsepower, would drive the ship at its cruise speed of twenty to twenty-five miles per hour. A secondary reserve engine of two hundred horsepower was for use in headwinds, while a third engine, ten horsepower, was used to drive an air pump. The vessel was equipped with fuel for fifty days and provisions for thirty. She set off in fog, and by the following day—October 16, 1910—reported a position some 300 miles from Atlantic City, east of Nantucket Island and the Massachusetts shore, cruising at a speed of eleven miles per hour.

Bad weather caused the flight to be abandoned, but not before Wellman set an endurance record of seventy-two hours, the longest a dirigible had been aloft at the time. There were several reasons for abandonment—motor trouble, lifting trouble, which meant that gasoline had to be dumped to maintain altitude, and difficulties in stabilizing the dirigible in the weather. Radio played an important part in the rescue by the steamship *Trent*, which finally picked up the airship some 250 miles northwest of Bermuda.

Just before World War I broke out, Auguste Piccard and his twin brother, Jean Felix, made their first ascension from Switzerland, flying over Germany to a landing in France. This was the beginning of a family fascination with balloons lasting to the present day.

The brothers continued their flying during the war, serving in the Swiss militia as Lighter-Than-Air Service pilots. At war's end, Jean left Switzerland for the United States to pursue his scientific career, which included high-altitude research. His brother accepted a position as professor of physics at Brussels University.

The two brothers had long been interested in aerostation. As early as 1905, they designed the world's first pressurized gondola, intended for high-altitude research. It was to be built in 1930, when Auguste obtained funds from the *Fonds National de Recherches Scientifiques* for a stratospheric ascent.

The experience of Captain Hawthorne Gray, a leading American balloonist of the 1920s, made it imperative that the Piccard balloon be built. Gray had taken second place in the 1926 Gordon–Bennet races and was anxious to break the world's altitude record. A serious person who was not about to take unnecessary risks, he felt he could do it in an open basket using the latest type of oxygen equipment. In 1927 he broke the existing record with a flight to 42,000 feet. But to achieve this altitude, he had thrown out all his ballast. When the time came to start his descent, he valved off some gas. But he must have valved too much, for the descent grew faster and faster, and was soon 900 feet per minute, or a little over ten miles per hour, and Gray decided to jump. He landed safely enough, but the rules say the aeronaut must return with the balloon, so technically, no record was set.

On November 4, 1927, Gray made ready for another ascent, from Scott Field, Illinois. At 40,000 feet the temperature was 40 degrees below zero, and the gondola and instruments were icing up. Gray found it difficult to record observations in his notebook. The ascent had been slower than originally planned, and with the clock freezing, there was no way for him to check how long he'd been up. He kept rising, and the barograph gave a maximum reading of 42,470 feet before the descent began. When the balloon landed, Gray was found dead—proving that pressurization is the only way to fly in rarified air.

some sixteen miles) where his main parachute deployed. A new record was set six years later when Nick Piantandia jumped out at 123,500 feet.

Two navy officers of the Strato-Lab program, Commander Malcolm D. Ross and Lieutenant Commander Victor A. Prather, ascended to 113,733 feet before coming down. Their record was marred after splashdown when Prather missed a sling from a helicopter and drowned. His heavy space suit dragged him beneath the waves.

Tracy Barnes is another person exploring new areas of aerostation. On May 26, 1973, he made the first flight in an aircraft totally powered by solar energy. *Solar Firefly* is a 200,000-cubic-foot tetroon (inflated tetrahedron) with which he expects to make stratospheric flights in the future. Barnes holds a number of FAI (Fédération Aéronautique Internationale) Diplômes de Record, special awards for ascents of 38,650 feet and 28,585 feet.

Maverick capitalist Malcolm Forbes made his first balloon ascension in June 1972, and was so delighted with the experience that it turned into the first of a number of instruction sessions that led to his FAA commercial license some five months later.

In October 1973, he set six official world records in hot-air ballooning, while becoming the first person in history to successfully fly coast-to-coast across America in a hot-air balloon. This was *Château de Balleroy*, which takes its name from the Forbes-owned Normandy château in France, where Forbes has established the world's first balloon museum. *Château de Balleroy* was designed by the father of modern hot-air ballooning, Ed Yost.

Château de Balleroy, the world's first $25,000 hot-air balloon, has a fifty-eight-foot diameter, sixty-five-foot height and a capacity of 95,000 cubic feet of hot air. The ultimate hot-air balloon, the secret of its design lies in the special inner layer of aluminized fabric which helps retain the heat, allowing almost twenty hours aloft. The aluminum backing inside permits heat retention by reflecting heat rays back into the center.

Forbes, who flew the machine to more than 17,000 feet on his record-breaking attempt across America, commented that there was more than enough warm air floating back down the throat of the balloon to keep him warm at that altitude.

Born in Englewood, New Jersey, in 1919, Forbes launched the most sophisticated program to develop a balloon that would cross the Atlantic. Launch date for *Windborne*, a multiple balloon project designed to support a pressurized gondola at jet-stream altitude of 40,000 feet, was set for December 30, 1974.

There have been a number of unsuccessful transatlantic attempts

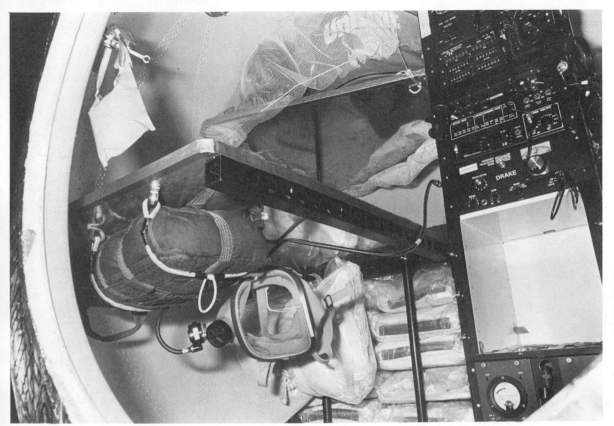

Interior of space-age gondola, a spherical capsule designed by the Neu-shall Corporation, Gardena, Ca., for the Forbes' Windborne *transatlantic bid. The central stack houses communications equipment to provide capsule-to-satellite-to-ground voice networking over entire route.*

throughout history. The first was in 1859, by Messrs. Haddock and La Montaigne, who made a brief, but fatal ascension from Watertown, New York. The second was by Thaddeus Lowe in 1860, from Reservoire Square, New York, but the aerostat was wrecked on inflation. The third, on October 6, 1873, with Captain W. H. Donaldson in command, was discussed previously.

The next crossing was not attempted until eighty-five years later, when *Small World*, crewed by four Britishers, lifted off from the Canary Islands on December 12, 1958, bound for the West Indies. They traveled 1,200 miles in four days before a storm forced them down into the high seas. In their seaworthy gondola they sailed the remaining 1,500 miles to Barbados, arriving on January 5, 1959. Two more unsuccessful attempts were made on the east-west route, using the trade winds.

August 10, 1968, saw two Canadians, Mark Winters and Jerry Kostur, ascend from Halifax, Nova Scotia, bound for Europe. They flew for fifty miles before being driven down to the seas by unfavorable weather. Both were rescued. On September 20, 1970, British balloonist Malcolm Brighton, along with stockbroker Rodney Anderson and his wife, Pamela, lifted off from East Hampton, Long Island, in *Free Life*, a hot-air balloon. Heavy rain off the coast of Newfoundland brought them down. Nothing but their picnic cooler was found after a five-day search.

There have also been other, more recent and unsuccessful flights.

The Forbes flight was to be different. As Forbes said at the time, "Survival will be an important concern of this project. We have a team of dedicated scientists and experts who have been working for many months on the design, construction and testing of every conceivable aspect of this venture. . . . I enjoy being alive," he added.

The key to survival at the planned altitude of 40,000 feet was a pressurized living space. Neushall Corporation of Gardena, California, designed a perfect sphere of aluminum, stretch-formed to just .023 inches thick, yet strong enough to withstand more than eight times the operating pressure. Insulating material to a thickness of 2.4 inches, covered by a thin aluminized plastic film was designed to keep interior temperature within the range of 40°F to 80°F.

Because of a total weight limitation of 4,000 pounds, the gondola is hardly spacious for one, let alone two people. Forbes was accompanied by Dr. Thomas Heinsheimer, a balloon enthusiast and a Fellow of the British Interplanetary Society. Multipositional bunks that could be raised to become either lounges or chairs were provided for sleeping. Food was developed by the U.S. Army. Personal hygiene consisted of brief "wash-ups" with sealed moist towelettes, use of a mechanical shaver and a chewable dentifrice. Urine was to be collected during the day in a container and jettisoned at night. Solid wastes were to be treated with a germicide and deodorants and placed in sealed containers for disposal on landing.

The proposed flight profile of the trip was of particular interest if only because the transatlantic flight was to start from California. There was good reason for this apparent madness, since it would give both ground crews and those flying the mission an opportunity to evaluate all systems, prior to the "wet" portion of the journey. According to calculations, *Windborne* would have made the U.S. continental crossing in twenty-four to forty-eight hours, to a probable landing in southern France or northern Africa in a total elapsed time of from four to seven days. Should any system have malfunctioned, the flight would have been aborted over land. And even if they'd had to ditch in the Atlantic, there were plenty of survival devices to see them through until rescue.

In addition to the immense amount of planning, there was the usual gallimaufry of scientific data collection that is commonplace these days on such expeditions. Included were some ten major atmospheric experiments sponsored by NASA (National Aeronautics and Space Administration), UCLA (University of California at Los Angeles), CNRS (France's National Center for Scientific Research) and *Forbes'* magazine's own Atlantic project.

The communications system aboard *Windborne* was among the most sophisticated aboard any private aircraft. Normal VHF (Very High Frequency) provided voice communication over land, with HF and VHF over water. For navigation, VOR and Loran (a special low-frequency band navigational signal) and sextant gave position as determined by the crew. But the addition of SMS (Synchronous Meteorological Satellite) to the system—which includes six transit satellites which passed round the earth every ninety minutes—meant the possibility of constantly updated positional data from *Windborne*. [The SMS link went as follows: *Windborne* to SMS, to NOAA (National Oceanographic and Atmospheric Administration) at Wallops Island, Virginia, to RCA Central Globcom (Global Communications) in New York City.]

There was perhaps only one problem—the Forbes attempt would be the thirteenth venture into the unknown. Forbes and Dr. Tom Heinsheimer dismissed that as so much superstition. They were armed with the very latest aerospace technology, possessed a ten-year study of the winds in the jet stream where they'd be flying, and there was no reason to suppose that with such a battery of communications equipment and survival gear there would be any trouble.

Originally the space pod was to be supported by twelve small helium-filled balloons, but then a thirteenth was added. Inflated to a greater degree than the others, it was located at the top of a stack of four tiers of three balloons each. Its primary purpose was to serve as pressure relief for the remaining helium-filled balloons, since if it should burst, it would simply bring *Windborne* to a lower altitude.

The flight was originally scheduled for December 1974. Delays occurred until January on account of weather, but finally the project got the word Go for a launching in the chill, early hours of Monday, January 6, 1975.

Several hundred spectators had gathered to see the 4:00 A.M. departure. As the ground crew shivered, Forbes and Tom Heinsheimer cheerfully shouted: "See you in Paris," before strapping themselves inside the pressurized gondola. The helium was started, but the lift and the wind caused problems. The upper balloons were whipping around the central column so that they could not be deflated anymore from inside. The ground equipment proved too weak to hold the gondola, which broke its moorings, dragging it some twenty feet before French aerospace scientist Jean Pierre

Pommereau—at considerable risk to himself—cut it loose, saving the gondola from an explosion of its store of liquid oxygen.

Forbes emerged shaken. "The most expensive twenty-foot trip in history," he told reporters with a laugh. The project would be delayed, indefinitely, he said, until the systems had been checked. But he expected it would be about six weeks before another launch could be attempted.

Later that week a press release issued from the Forbes office said the project would be delayed by nearly a year on account of the jet stream. But then the Atlantic project was indefinitely suspended. Forbes said he was going to wait until a new balloon material had been perfected, which he reckoned would be some time in 1977. He felt that the single-balloon concept was more valid, and on a model demonstrated how they nearly had lost their lives. They had no means of getting down once the wind had whipped the balloon cables around the main shaft, since the internal detonating systems wouldn't have freed the balloons.

The most recent, and American bicentennial contender, Karl Thomas, age 27, suffered extremely bad weather and a communications breakdown, and had to bail out in the North Atlantic. He was picked up by a Soviet trawler with three broken ribs. His wife reported a successful recovery and his return to his general aviation business in Troy, Michigan.

A Look into the Future of Aerostation

*T*he future of balloons and dirigibles as a means of serious transportation seemed doomed on May 6, 1937, when Germany's aerial flagship *Hindenburg*—the world's largest dirigible—was ripped apart by an explosion that sent her crumpling onto the naval landing field at Lakehurst, New Jersey, where she was docking, killing one-third of all the passengers aboard. The *Hindenburg* exploded because she was filled with hydrogen gas, not the helium that she was designed to carry. Had the oil interests that controlled the helium gas fields of Kansas, New Mexico, Texas and Utah been willing to sell their gas, this horror would have probably been avoided.

While balloons have been used in a relatively desultory manner for obtaining weather information, for long-term meteorological observations and for advertising, lighter-than-air vehicles have been kept out of the public eye for years in favor of more costly alternatives which yield Big Business greater profits—usually at the expense of the general public.

If accelerating fuel costs have meant greater profits for the oil corporations and bigger handouts to their lobbyists in the Congresses and Parliaments around the world, this fact has also raised serious questions about the cost-effectiveness of air-cargo transport. For several years, enthusiasts in America, England and the Soviet Union have been working on superairships capable of carrying far more than the ninety tons of cargo a 747 superjet can carry—and do it more efficiently and economically to boot.

Apart from issues of economy and effectively using what fuel remains untapped in the bowels of the earth, public concern for the environment— also a dwindling resource in America—has changed many people's thinking about whether giant jets (which gulp down fuel at even more extravagant rates than the behemoths of Detroit's drawing boards) are even desirable fixtures in our skies. For the airlines have permitted the spawning of one of the fastest developing bureaucracies of all—the Federal Aviation Administration, most of whose work consists of freeing the skies from private aircraft for the benefit of the airlines, the military, and the upper echelons of business. Someone has to pay for this, and again, it is the general public.

As nations become more aware of the reality of the energy crisis, it seems likely that there will be a call for a reinvestigation into the use of airships. With modern technology to provide a design safety factor they never enjoyed in their heyday, airships would really make a great deal more sense than either aircraft or superships. Certainly history has shown that they were considerably ahead of their time. And there is little doubt that had the *Hindenburg* been filled with helium rather than hydrogen, its destruction would not have occurred.

Traveling in an airship the size of the *Hindenburg* was akin to traveling aboard a luxurious mini ocean liner. About the only thing that made it different (other than the view) was that smoking was only permitted in a special room because of the danger of an explosion. There was an elegant restaurant, a ballroom floor, showers, private cabins and even a panoramic viewing platform. Crossing the Atlantic took fifty to sixty hours in incredible comfort, with none of the tossing of either modern sea or air travel and, consequently, no motion sickness.

And if you lost an engine, there was really nothing to worry about— it would just take a bit longer. You had all the lift you required in the bag. And in terms of fuel economy, it beats the 747 jumbo jet hands down.

In November 1975, Congress got a first look at a House resolution introduced by Representative George E. Brown, Jr. (D–Calif.) urging the federal government to "accelerate its investigation, development, demonstration of, and research on lighter-than-air systems." Brown, who has a track record as one of the more serious fuel conservationists in the House of Representatives, has also introduced other measures to promote or reintroduce such items as bicycles, electric cars, solar heaters and wind generators. Along with a reinvestigation into lighter-than-air vehicles, the Brown resolution calls for a new look at sailing ships; this measure is sure to displease certain interest groups that seem to be rather powerful in our country today.

Brown's point is well taken, since both airships and sailing vessels use niggardly amounts of fossil fuels in comparison with their fuel-intensive counterparts the energy industries have foisted on us, ladled in chrome, for the profitability of their suppliers. As Brown himself says: "Lighter-than-air craft have low fuel consumption and minimal adverse environmental impact, especially in comparison to heavier-than-air craft." He also pointed out—and rightly so—that airships are uniquely suited for carrying large indivisible loads, and unlike jumbos, airships do not need enormous runways and expensive cargo-handling systems on the ground.

Brown's opponents point out that where speed is of the essence, the jumbo 747 can make six trips to an airship's one, and when speed is not a factor, contemporary steamships can haul cargo with greater reliability—if not greater fuel economy—than airships. But there is always this question of fuel efficiency, especially if fuel is running out so fast that we have to raise prices to reduce consumption. It seems likely that given airships' potential freight capacity, refrigerated storage could provide the necessary ingredient to maintain the freshness of items requiring speedier transportation. All things considered, the superjet proponents seem to be speaking for the need to feed profits to Big Oil.

That Washington, D.C.'s entrenched bureaucracy will even bother to lift a finger and take effective action seems unlikely. We have already noted its strictly public-relations approach to the demands of the electorate, the pusillanimous dance to outside strings which dole out billions of dollars to nuclear (and military) interests, while appropriating minuscule amounts for solar research.

As for Congress, unless there are serious changes in the priorities of its membership, little more than the traditional clichés will be heard to reassure that handful of critical voters out in the hinterland. And then once again, it will be business as usual.

At the present time, Canada has an interesting program underway. A joint private and government program is financing a $1.3-million project to build a 120-foot-long blimp with a three-quarter-ton payload. The first one will be ready for tests early in 1977, and if successful, a larger model will be built.

In the late 1960s, a group of New Jersey businessmen decided to see whether they could build a replica of Solomon Andrews's *Aereon*, which originally flew more than 100 years ago. Their reason for delving into the past was that *Aereon* was like a sailing ship and could fly directly into the wind, though it apparently used the force of gravity.

As mentioned earlier, the New Jersey prototype was a full-sized ship with an auxiliary motor, and it flew quite well. However, the group was unable to raise money to build a large cargo ship, and the project was put aside.

In the Soviet Union, work is now being done on the use of giant dirigibles to assist in the development of Siberia, much of which remains uninhabited. Siberia, for so long a place of exile for dissenters, has turned out to be one of the greater treasure troves of the planet. Airships may be just one of the tools used to open up this territory, since an airfield servicing dirigibles takes little time to prepare compared to one necessary for large cargo aircraft.

The Soviets have had a design team of more than 100 engineers studying the feasibility of airships since 1960. In the early 1960s they produced plans for a sort of aerial trimaran, an airship with three hulls, but this was later discarded for a more traditional design. In 1968, wind-tunnel testing on a scale model 100-passenger, 110-mile-per-hour design was begun. Known as the D–1, it is believed to be a prototype of an airship freighter to ship matériel to the fifty Soviet military divisions assigned to the Sino-Soviet border.

In France, the government is actively researching airships as a means of moving the large components used in setting up nuclear power stations. European nations, with less land mass and with neighboring nation states to contend with, have pursued nuclear plant safety much more diligently than America's industry has. Airships, because of their capacity to move large indivisible loads, such as the giant castings used in nuclear plant technology, may thus be a key to greater nuclear safety. This is clearly an example of an old technology helping a newer one.

The British have been looking at airships for some time to service their North Sea oil platforms less expensively. Most oil rigs are serviced by helicopters which, while efficient, are expensive to build, run and maintain. On the average, a helicopter requires a half-hour on land for every hour it is in operation; airships require a fraction of this down time, are relatively cheap to build, and are also cost- and fuel-effective.

The British have had much practical experience in this field, having used balloons and blimps in two World Wars, and having redeveloped the Zeppelin-type dirigible between the wars. Advocates in England claim that the potential of dirigibles as cargo carriers was deliberately stifled by special-interest groups more concerned with the development of less fuel-efficient machines.

Some years ago, a firm called Manchester Liners Ltd.—a subsidiary of the Furness–Withy group, whose wealth was founded on shipping—proposed plans for the development of giant dirigibles which would provide a worldwide air-cargo service. Their proposal called for the development of 1,200-foot-long air freighters with a maximum speed of 100 miles per hour and a cargo capacity of 500 tons of containerized freight. According to the figures at the time, the cost of shipping freight would be little more than surface rates with the additional advantage of a speed some five to seven times faster than more conventional shipping. The freight would be carried within the hull of the airship in twenty-foot bulk containers and would be off-loaded from the cargo vessel by a team of Sikorsky S–64 helicopters, which have a lifting capability of thirty-eight tons. Helicopters would be used instead of more conventional means of unloading because airships would never land, seldom moor and almost never come to a complete halt except for a major overhaul. A minimum air speed of around twenty-five miles per hour would be sufficient to keep the ship aloft, using additional lifting (or downward thrust) propellers around the hull's midsection.

Manchester Liners Ltd. grew and changed ownership, and former journalist Max Rynish became managing director of Cargo Airships Ltd., their subsidiary. Rynish succeeded in arousing serious interest in the commercial practicability of cargo airships.

In the mid-1960s, Professor Francis Morse proposed a nuclear powered airship. The Morse-type atomic airship would provide nonpolluting air cruising with virtually unlimited range—similar to nuclear submarines. London to New York would be about forty hours, and New York to Paris an hour or two longer. Above all, no new airports or runways would be required, and unlike Concorde, there would be no additional noise.

Unlike regular aircraft, where atomic power is ruled out by the weight of the shielding, there is no such problem in an airship. The weight of the reactor with its shielding would be around 100,000 pounds, which is not very much when considered against a gross lift of nearly 800,000 pounds at 95 percent of gross lift.

There is, of course, a radiation hazard. But unlike conventional aircraft, airships are highly maneuverable at any speed and, except for landing, can fly above all serious forms of weather. The comfort of modern pressurization takes care of that. So, if there were storms at the landing area, the airship could either wait until they passed or divert to another airport where the weather was better. But there would be none of the anxiety associated with the business of finding an alternate.

And if there was heavy fog, because of its ability to reduce speed to a walking pace if necessary and descend very slowly, the airship could easily make zero-zero landings. In the early days, Zeppelins and dirigibles were regularly making landings of this sort, despite the lack of instrument landing systems.

The point is that unlike regular aircraft, the airship is actually incredibly safe. The only problem would be to ensure that either a military

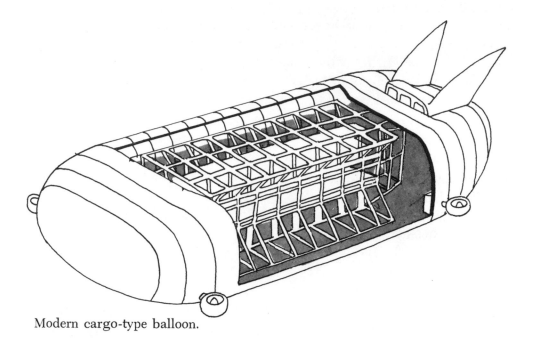

Modern cargo-type balloon.

or foreign-made reactor were fitted to it, since U.S. made reactors, which have had so many corners cut in the name of bigger profit, may present more of a potential health hazard.

Worldwide inflation has made nonsense of the projected figures for the operation, but some of the basic data—such as an estimated one percent loss of helium per month—are still valid, and even now may be improved upon. Max Rynish also pointed out the advantages of using natural gas from the recently developed North Sea rigs as fuel, since it would be more efficient in terms of weight and less polluting than conventional fuels. Then there's the question of trim (balance): Rynish proposed to go back to basics—the old airship way—by storing the water that condensed in the exhaust outlet tubes. This old-fashioned method was so efficient that for 100 pounds of fuel burned, 100 pounds of water was collected. Additional ballast (and fresh water) came from rain collection. The superheating of helium would be another method of maintaining trim, by altering the density of helium, which won't burn or explode.

Modern materials such as titanium alloy or even carbon fiber, if inexpensive enough, would serve for the framework of the new generation of airships. Outer skins would be lightweight synthetics, designed to add a monocoque-style rigidity to the entire structure.

Advocates on this side of the Atlantic agree. L. R. Hackney of Southern California's Aviation Council LTA Task Force foresees single shipments of over 300 tons as practical. And William L. Kitterman, a lighter-than-air enthusiast with the government's Energy Research and Development Administration, feels that by combining developing materials with existing technology there is the potential "to build something on the order of a 75-million-cubic-foot airship." A 750-ton payload would be reasonable for such a vehicle, and Kitterman believes that if we can build the bigger versions, then smaller scale LTA cargos of twenty-five or fifty million cubic feet are not only possible, but "they can move cargo and passengers much more efficiently and economically than we are moving them now."

Then there are the hybrid schemes. One of these is a design by Frank N. Piasecki, president of Piasecki Aircraft Corporation, which calls for a centralized lifting pod, coupled by a trellis structure to four Sikorsky CH–53D helicopters. Originated as a heavy assault and transport helicopter like the CH–53A, the 53D developed from a long line of large helicopters which began with the Sikorsky S–60 and later became a pure cargo aircraft.

Piasecki's *Heli-Stat* would carry a seventy-five-ton payload, making it highly useful for transporting heavy tank equipment around a battlefield. It could also be developed to shift the space shuttle from point to point in the United States, though it is likely that a pure dirigible might do this job better.

Not everyone is sanguine on the subject, and dirigibles have more than their share of doomsayers. The military is not enamored with them, since they are relatively easy to destroy and difficult to protect. Moreover, in general, the military has not been very successful with them, although the navy—which decommissioned its last LTA squadron in 1961—is still considering the use of blimps for a number of assignments, including supporting radar platforms tethered at 70,000 feet to acquire weather data, and for antisubmarine work as well as equipment-carrying to offshore facilities. But it was largely thanks to a navy grant that contemporary hot-air ballooning was reborn and now provides enthusiasts with an inexpensive and enjoyable way to experience the skies of our land.

Raven Industries, which brought about this revolution, is looking into the potential missions for hot-air soft dirigibles. Such tasks presently accomplished at greater expense by helicopter, such as traffic patrols, pipeline patrols and so forth are definitely feasible. Current speeds in the low fifties, might make the project impractical on a windy day, but there's no doubt about the savings in operating costs and maintenance, according to the manufacturers.

And what of the future?

Balloonists are moderately competitive, and a number of tasks in precision altitude keeping are popular at meets.

There seems a good possibility of a return to the airship as a means of stretching dwindling supplies of fossil fuels. With the development of inexpensive solar cells providing instant electricity from sunlight, an electric airship might well become feasible, since it could use its vast surface area for transforming sunlight into power. (Even on cloudy days these cells still generate a small current, and while currently too expensive for ordinary citizens, they are being used by the military and the telephone company to power repeater stations in rural areas. The same types of devices provided electrical power to the NASA projects.)

The original airships required complicated and heavy skeletons, latticeworks of girders and complex rigging, all of which had to be primitively sealed with old-fashioned fabric. The engines that powered these early giants were nowhere near as efficient as modern ones in terms of their weight-to-horsepower ratio; consequently, the early airships were left to the mercy of the elements. A further drawback at that time was the use of hydrogen instead of helium as the lifting gas. Apart from a small amount in experimental use today, helium is mostly being released to the atmosphere by

Happiness is a sky filled with beautiful aerostats.

the oil companies, since it isn't profitable to store it. Unfortunately, oil companies are not noted for their public spirit.

In addition to the rising price of fuel, another reason that air freight has not burgeoned to the degree its proponents predicted in the early 1950s is that in order to double the load in a conventional fixed-wing aircraft, it is necessary to cube the amount of thrust its engines produce and lengthen the runway. In terms of engineering, extra fuel and the increased price of the engines, this costs a great deal of money. You must also budget the increase in the length of the runway required for the larger machinery, but the FAA will usually overlook that in their cost-accounting, at the expense of private aviation.

Lighter-than-air vessels are very different. If you want to double the payload, you need less than double the vehicle's overall size. You do not require a much larger unloading area, and runways are no problem at all.

A further advantage of airships compared with conventional aircraft is that since they carry their own lift, they require much smaller engines.

Thus, in addition to using less fuel, they are also quieter. And because they produce less exhaust gas, they cause less pollution.

A conventional aircraft has the disadvantage that much of its thrust must be used to achieve lift from its wings, even with special high-lift (high-cost technology) devices to aid it at low speeds. In the case of airships, this problem is minimized. To put it another way, let's say it takes 1,000 horse-power to move one ton in a conventional aircraft. An airship would require only 200 horsepower, since the lifting capacity is already built in with the gas. This makes it more than four times as efficient as a fixed-wing aircraft.

The real reason the airship has not been developed is because it is easy to shoot down, and has few military uses. But for a future world which is more sane and where politicians are genuinely interested in the welfare of all people, the airship will make remarkably good sense. It is labor-intensive and relatively cheap to run, and once there is the technology for its construction, it can be made on license almost anywhere in the world. Even the oil companies should be pleased, since a return to the airship would mean an outlet for all their excess helium.

And if we insist on putting nuclear reactors into aircraft, then an airship is by far the most reasonable craft in which to install it, since the motor can easily be separated from passengers and crew, with considerably less shielding (and less weight) than in a hypothetical, conventional fixed-wing machine.

Finally, because of their slow speeds and ability to near-hover if necessary, airships are not prone to high-speed, body-splattering, violent impacts which transform those elegant winged aluminum tubes into the nightmares that front-page news stories have revealed in our times. As for the weather accidents of yore, our contemporary radar should pretty much eliminate them.

Will airships be developed in America again? Right now it seems more likely they will be developed again elsewhere. American industrialists are noted more for profiteering than innovation, and our bureaucracy is too responsive to the needs of minority interests.

Lewis Mumford summed it up a long time ago: "The primary purpose of transportation is not to increase the amount of physical movement, but to increase the possibilities of human association, cooperation, personal communication, and choice." Our society, it seems to me, has yet to elect to choose those systems—in transportation or elsewhere—that provide the maximum benefit and are within the reach of the majority. Whether we're aeronauts or not, we ignore this idea at our peril.

Appendices

Where to Find Flight Training

(listed alphabetically by state)

United States

Bud Langford
Route 6, Box 361
Jonesboro, Arkansas   72401

Marvin Altman
Route 2, Box 60
Van Buren, Arkansas   72956

David G. Robinson
P.O. Box 2978
Castro Valley, California   94546

Brent Stockwell
777 Beachwood Drive
Daly City, California   94015

Daedelus School of Free Ballooning
Menlo Oaks Balloon Field
Menlo Park, California   94025

Fred Krieg
246 Lomita Drive
Box 1147
Perris, California   92370

Chauncey M. Dunn
4643 Wadsworth
Denver, Colorado   80033

Bill Costen
105 Sherbrooke Ave.
Hartford, Connecticut   06106

Kingswood Sprott, Jr.
P.O. Box 2736
Lakeland, Florida   33803

The Indiana Aeronaut Academy
P.O. Box 2634
Anderson, Indiana   46011

Tom Gabel Balloons
110 South Cottage Grover
Urbana, Illinois   61802

Tom Oerman
American Balloons Services, Inc.
113 Park Avenue
Muscatine, Iowa   52761

Henry "Red" Horrocks
Nevermore Balloon Sales
1307 Lee Lane
Sykesville, Maryland   21784

Ralph Hall
1656 Massachusetts Avenue
Lexington, Massachusetts   02170

Dr. Clayton Thomas
Balloon School of Massachusetts
RFD 1, Dingley Dell
Palmer, Massachusetts   01069

Douglas N. Mills
6146 Thornapple River Drive
Alto, Michigan   49302

Dennis Floden
American Aeropromotion
Flint, Michigan   48502

Wiederkehr Balloon Flight Training
1604 Euclid Street
St. Paul, Minnesota   55106

Balloon Ascensions Ltd.
Route 11, Box 279
Statesville, North Carolina   28677

Rodger Kell
1121 East 7th Street
Plainfield, New Jersey   07062

Sky Promotions Flight Training
20 Nassau Street
Princeton, New Jersey   08540

Sid Cutter
World Balloon Championships, Inc.
3323 Princeton Drive N.E.
Albuquerque, New Mexico   87107

Ron Edwards
611 Button Road
Chittenango, New York   13064

Sam Cali
Greenbush Aviation
45 Highland Avenue
East Greenbush, N.Y.   12061
(near Albany)

Jerry Hacker
34 Beach Front Lane
New Rochelle, New York   10805

Chalet Club
Jim Thorne
116 East 30th Street
New York, New York   10016

Bill Hughes
Box 3130
Poughkeepsie, New York   12602

Jim Benson
Cloud 9 Promotions
4 Velox Street
Rochester, New York   14615

Tim Forte
Balloon Adventures
106 Forest Avenue, Apt. E
Narberth, Pennsylvania   19072
(near Philadelphia)

Rod Harris
855 Tioque Avenue
Coventry, Rhode Island   02816

Southwestern Balloon School
503 East 46th Street
Austin, Texas   78751

Rainbow's End Balloon Port
Route 9, Box 805
Houston, Texas   77040

Mike Choucalas
Balloon Promotions
P.O. Drawer 210
Midland, Texas   79701

Bob Wadds
10 Acres Lodge
RR 1
Stowe, Vermont   05673

AERIE Balloon Enterprises
1510 12th Street North, Room 603
Arlington, Virginia   22209

Steve Hoffman
Barnstormer Airshows, Inc.
Hangar #2
Hanover Municipal Airport
Ashland, Virginia   23005

Ted W. Parod
P.O. Box 348
Lynden, Washington   98264

Aloft Ltd.
P.O. Box 78214
Seattle, Washington   98178

Canada

Larry Horack
Flight Systems
306 Euclid Street

Whitby, Ontario LIN 5B6
Canada

Balloon Makers and Their Products

Cameron Balloons Ltd. (England)
1 Chotham Park
Bristol BS6 6BZ
England

Cameron Balloons
3600 Elizabeth Road
Ann Arbor, Michigan   48103

Model	Crew	F.A.I. Category	Burner Rating (BTU per hr)	Fuel Volume (Stand. Tanks) (gal.)	Diameter (ft.)	Overall Height (ft.)	Volume (cu. ft.)	System Wt. With Full Fuel (lbs.)	Max. Certified Lift (Payload) (lbs. at sea level)	Price
O-31	1	AX-4	15,000,000	20	41	54	31,450	351	630	$4,120
O-42	2	AX-5	15,000,000	20	45½	59	42,000	380	840	$4,630
O-56	2	AX-6	15,000,000	20	50	65	56,000	435	1120	$5,130
O-65	3	AX-7	15,000,000	30	52½	68	65,000	558	1300	$5,650
O-77	4	AX-7	15,000,000	40	56	72	77,500	645	1550	$6,130
O-84	4	AX-8	15,000,000	40	57	74	84,000	650	1680	$6,330
A-105	6	AX-8	30,000,000	60	62	80	105,000	882	2100	$7,650
A-140	8	AX-9	30,000,000	80	68	88	140,000	1072	2800	$8,610
D-96	2	NA	30,000,000	40	100 Long	50	96,000	NA	1920	$14,400

Don Piccard Balloons, Inc.
P.O. Box 1902
Newport Beach, California   92663

Model	Crew	F.A.I. Category	Burner Rating (BTU per hr)	Fuel Volume (Stand. Tanks) (gal.)	Diameter (ft.)	Overall Height (ft.)	Volume (cu. ft.)	System Wt. With Full Fuel (lbs.)	Max. Certified Lift (Payload) (lbs. at sea level)	Price
AX-6C	1–2	AX-5	12,000,000	20	40	50	42,000	350	800	$5,375
AX-6R	2–3	AX-6	12,000,000	20–30	50	60	56,000	395	1000	$5,875
AX-6W	3	AX-7	25,000,000	40	55	70	77,000	475	1210	$6,375

Mike Adams Balloon Loft
P.O. Box 12168
Atlanta, Georgia   30306

Model	Crew	F.A.I. Category	Burner Rating (BTU per hr)	Fuel Volume (Stand. Tanks) (gal.)	Diameter (ft.)	Overall Height (ft.)	Volume (cu. ft.)	System Wt. With Full Fuel (lbs.)	Max. Certified Lift (Payload) (lbs. at sea level)	Price
A-50/AX-6	2–3						55,000			$4,800
A-50S/AX-7	3						62,000			$5,200
A-55/AX-7	3–4						75,000			$5,700
A-55S/AX-8	4						83,000			$6,200

Raven Industries, Inc.
Balloon Group Box 1007
Sioux Falls, South Dakota   57101

Model	Crew	F.A.I. Category	Burner Rating (BTU per hr)	Fuel Volume (Stand. Tanks) (gal.)	Diameter (ft).	Overall Height (ft.)	Volume (cu. ft.)	System Wt. With Full Fuel (lbs.)	Max. Certified Lift (Payload) (lbs. at sea level)	Price
Rally RX-6	1–3	AX-6	11,000,000	20	50	58	56,400	395	1430*	$4,595
S 50-A	1–4	AX-6	11,000,000	30	50	58	56,400	465	1400*	$5,765
S 55-A	1–4	AX-7	11,000,000	30	55	63	77,500	490	1450*	$6,895
S 60-A	1–4	AX-8	11,000,000	30	60	69	105,400	520	1500*	$7,515

Semco Balloon
Route 3, Box 514
Aerodrome Way
Griffin, Georgia   30223

Model	Crew	F.A.I. Category	Burner Rating (BTU per hr)	Fuel Volume (Stand. Tanks) (gal.)	Diameter (ft).	Overall Height (ft.)	Volume (cu. ft.)	System Wt. With Full Fuel (lbs.)	Max. Certified Lift (Payload) (lbs. at sea level)	Price
30AL	1	AX-4	2,000,000	19	40	60	30,000	258	462	$4,095
Model T	2	AX-6	4,000,000	22	50	68	53,000	341	640	$4,295
Mark V	2	AX-6	5,000,000	22	51	70	56,000	361	680	$4,695
Challenger	3	AX-7	8,000,000	22	52	70	75,750	381	880	$5,650
TC-4A	4	AX-8	8,000,000	44	55	82	91,000	515	1003	$6,495

The Balloon Works
Rhyne Aerodrome
RFD 2
Statesville, North Carolina   28677

Model	Crew	F.A.I. Category	Burner Rating (BTU per hr)	Fuel Volume (Stand. Tanks) (gal.)	Diameter (ft).	Overall Height (ft.)	Volume (cu. ft.)	System Wt. With Full Fuel (lbs.)	Max. Certified Lift (Payload) (lbs. at sea level)	Price
Fire Fly-7	NA	AX-7	21,000,000	30	55	58	77,000	500	1660	$8,250

Thunder Balloons Ltd.
75 Leonard Street
London EC2A 4QS
England

Model	Crew	F.A.I. Category	Burner Rating (BTU per hr)	Fuel Volume (Stand. Tanks) (gal.)	Diameter (ft.)	Overall Height (ft.)	Volume (cu. ft.)	System Wt. With Full Fuel (lbs.)	Max. Certified Lift (Payload) (lbs. at sea level)	Price
AX5/42	2	AX-5	6,000,000	20	44	57	42,000	400	919.8	$3,877
AX6/56	2–3	AX-6	6,000,000	20	48	63	56,000	425	1226.4	$4,112
AX6/56-A**	2–3	AX-6	6,000,000	20	48	62	56,000	437	1226.4	$4,406
AX7/65	3	AX-7	6,000,000	30	51	65	65,000	527	1423.5	$4,406
AX7/77	4	AX-7	6,000,000	40	54	70	77,000	625	1686.3	$4,688
AX7/77-A**	4	AX-7	6,000,000	40	54	69	77,000	643	1686.3	$5,052
AX8/105	6	AX-8	12,000,000	60	61	74	105,000	870	2299.5	$6,286
AX9/140	8	AX-9	12,000,000	80	67	81	140,000	1080	3066	$7,402

* Or lift at maximum envelope temperature of 250°.
** Parachute rip panel.

Preflight Checklist

Fuel
- Check quantity (normal training flights will start with all tanks filled to capacity)
- Install tank-checking security
- Clear fuel lines
- Connect and test fuel system for leaks

Burner system operational check
- Pilot valve
- Cruise valve
- Blast valve

Loading
- Determine gross weight
- Determine altitude limitation

Check deflation port closed
Check temperature telltales
Check maneuvering vent sealed
Instruments checked and secured
- Altimeter
- Variometer
- Pyrometer
- Compass

Drag line aboard and secured (drag lines are hardly ever used in hot-air balloons)
Igniters (two minimum) checked and aboard
Check inflation fan operation

Inflation
Checklist

Position basket for proper fuel feed
Spread envelope out properly
Assign and brief ground crew
Perform cold inflation
Envelope check
- Fabric integrity
- Deflation port strap clear
- Maneuvering vent line clear
- Recheck to see that deflation port and maneuvering vent are sealed

Use burner to inflate to upright position
Aborting inflation
- Open deflation port with rip strap
- Maintain crew positions until envelope completely deflates
- To reinflate, return to first step of inflation

Pre–Lift-off Checklist

Secure maneuvering vent line and deflation port strap to basket
Recheck fabric integrity, vent and port
Fuel selection
- Draw fuel from each source
- Select fullest tank
- Insure tank valves are either full-on or full-off

Adjust pilot light and cruise valve as needed
Instruments
- Set altimeter
- Turn on variometer and set to "0"
- Check pyrometer operation

Set pressure regulator
Check to see that ground handling lines and tether ropes are free
Recheck to see that minimum of two functioning igniters are aboard
Protective headgear for all occupants

Lift-off Checklist

Normal
Obtain equilibrium
Check and note pyrometer reading
Check that ground crew and spectators are clear
Using blast valve, proceed with lift-off with sufficient rate of climb to clear all obstacles (initial rate of heating should be high to insure safe lift-off with regard to possible false lift and wind shift or increase in velocity).
Monitor pyrometer and variometer
With Positive Buoyancy (to overcome obstacles or compensate for high wind or false lift) Use the same steps as in normal lift-off with the following additional steps:
- Brief two ground crew members only to hold the balloon down while additional heat over that required for equilibrium is applied (normally 20°F additional will suffice).
- On a predetermined positive signal from the pilot, the ground crew members will simultaneously release the balloon.

Landing Checklist

Preparation
- Position occupants side by side, facing the direction of movement, using up-wind structures for handholds
- Burners off prior to touchdown, release grip on burner controls, leave fuel tank valve and pilot light on
- Flex knees and cushion landing impact with legs

Touchdown in Light Winds
- Just prior to touchdown, open maneuvering vent, holding it open until ground travel ceases

Touchdown in High Winds and/or with Limited Ground Travel Clearances
- Simultaneously with touchdown, open deflation port as quickly as possible to its maximum
- Hold it from reclosing until ground travel has ceased, or longer if necessary

Water Landings
- In light winds, proceed with normal landing techniques and keep balloon inflated if possible
- In high winds:
    Position occupants so that they can exit to the side
    After impact, move all occupants outside
    Maintain position outside of basket, remaining with balloon; the basket will float and provide buoyancy

Post Touchdown
- Remain in the basket, keeping all parts of the body within the confines of it
- Stay as low as possible
- Remain clear of burners, fuel lines, and fittings
- Except in necessary emergencies, do not exit until it is determined that the balloon will remain stable while doing so.

Post Landing Checklist

Turn off fuel tanks and purge fuel lines
Turn off variometer
Reseal maneuvering vent and deflation port
Inspect envelope and basket for damage
Stow envelope

Gas Balloon

The envelope of a gas balloon is spherical in shape except for special mission balloon, which is enclosed by a net that in turn spreads the load of the gondola evenly over it.

Like the hot-air balloon, there is a ripping panel and a valve that can be used—much like the maneuvering vent of the hot-air balloon—to vent gas.

Unlike the hot-air balloon, the gas-type balloon carries ballast, usually bags of sand that serve to control the up/down motion of the balloon. It is used to counter the lifting power of the gas and during the flight is dispersed periodically to allow for the escape of gas and thus for a decrease in lift.

A gas balloon flight is over the moment the aeronaut reckons that the remaining ballast is sufficient only for landing. Landing a gas balloon is more difficult than a hot-air balloon and consists of the careful use of a guiderope or dragline—a cable of more than 100 meters: Its weight and frictional force provide a partial braking action and controllable ballast—the valve and the remaining ballast.

There is a move toward use of the flaccid type gas balloon, which is less expensive. But even these have drawbacks, especially during windy takeoffs. Both flaccid and rigid gas balloons require extreme care during inflation, and great care must be taken in *weighing* the balloon.

Glossary

aeronate Early term used to describe a captive balloon. See also **tether.**

aeronaut A person who operates or acts as crewperson in an aerostat. Also used colloquially to describe passengers in such vehicles.

aerostat A flying machine using a container filled with lighter-than-air gas (or hot air) and thus supported by its buoyancy relative to the air surrounding it.

aerostation The art (and science) of operating lighter-than-air vehicles.

airway An air corridor, so designated by the Federal Aviation Administration (FAA), controlled by Air Traffic Control (ATC) and marked by radio navigational beacons.

airworthy The state of any aircraft's being in a condition for safe flight.

altimeter An aneroid barometer, so arranged that it indicates the altitude of an aircraft above sea level by measuring air pressure and reading out the result in feet above sea level.

altitude Generally quoted in height in feet above mean sea level, altitude is also given as height above the ground over which an aircraft is flying—Above Ground Level, or AGL.

annual, annual inspection An inspection that must be completed every twelve months by an appropriately certificated mechanic to verify the condition of airworthiness of a flying machine. Certain work may be required to be done in order to bring a craft back into condition before an annual may be signed off if the owner is slipshod in caring for his vehicle.

apex The upper pole, "north" pole, or top center point of the balloon envelope.

apex line Fancy name for **crown line,** q.v.

approach The final stage in flight during which a flying machine transitions from an aerial to a ground environment. The approach precedes the actual landing, and is used to make sure the landing is effective.

ATC or Air Traffic Control Described by the FAA as a "service operated by appropriate authority to promote the safe, orderly and expeditious flow of air traffic." The concept of air traffic control from the ground is undergoing review in light of recent commercial flight accidents. The successful development of RNAV (radio navigation point-to-point) and Collision Avoidance devices makes its future most dubious.

attitude Describes a vehicle's position relative to the horizon.

ballast Weights—usually sandbags—used and carried in gas-type balloons to assist in maintaining a regular flight altitude and for descents. Hardly ever found in hot-air balloons.

balloon A lighter-than-air vehicle that derives its lift from either a specific gas—such as hydrogen, helium, or methane (coal gas)—or hot air. Used also to describe the envelope, a nonporous bag of tightly woven, strong material with a good resistance to heat and a minimum porosity—in the case of hot-air balloons. In gas balloons, usually of a high-grade plastic of petrochemical origin, such as Du Pont Mylar.

As Webster might put it: a nondirigible aerostat.

barograph A barometer, usually aneroid, that automatically records variations in atmospheric pressure—often as altitude or height above a mean point—on a revolving paper-covered cylinder.

basket See **gondola.** The carrying part of the balloon equipage, in which burner(s), controls, instruments, fuel and aeronauts are usually contained.

blast off High-speed ascension using positive buoyancy, used typically when there is a breeze and the aeronaut needs to make a speedy ascent. See also **weigh off.**

While there is also an amusement factor in viewing the balloon making a swift ascent, it takes longer for the pilot to take command of his altitude.

blast valve A flight burner override control which bypasses the regulator, sending full tank pressure through the burner system. It gives the pilot almost instant hot air on the new big burner (high BTU) systems. Also known as *joy valve* and *tooter*, the blast valve, when in use, produces the sort of noise an unsilenced home heating unit makes.

blimp A nonrigid, or semirigid airship.

burner A device for mixing propane or butane with air to produce a hot flame, being the primary heat source in hot-air balloons.

The device is normally made of a metal tube coiled round a venturi, at the mouth of which is placed a jet, or nozzle. The burner has two basic controls—a regulator valve, which may be adjusted upward to "cruise" output. See **cruise valve** and **blast valve.**

burner mount, platform, frame The burner is attached to a frame to secure it. More and more makers are opting for a rigid frame which is part of the gondola, rather than the free-floating burner mount. In addition to reducing the hazard of being hit on the head or igniting the envelope during a landing (from heat, since only the pilot light remains on), a fixed position also seems safer for inflation.

ceiling The height above ground of the base of cloud cover. Sometimes quoted as altitude Mean Sea Level (MSL).

checklist An itemized list of procedures. Also the safest way to ensure that you are operating your flying machine correctly.

cockpit Sometimes used to describe the area within the gondola of a balloon, usually by pilots of other types of air vehicles. Technically they're correct, since the word describes that part of a flying machine in which the pilot controls the aircraft.

cross-country Almost all balloon flights are cross-country flights. The term is used to designate a flight between two points by the FAA.

crown   Same as **apex**—top dead center of the balloon.

crown line   A rope attached to the **crown** of the balloon and used for ground handling during inflation, to prevent or diminish oscillation. On dumping balloons the crown line attaches to the gondola, and is used as a static line to invert the balloon.

cruise valve, regulator valve, metering valve, flight valve   An adjustable valve which controls the flow of fuel (propane or butane) through the burner regulator.

deflation port   Term sometimes used for **maneuvering vent,** q.v.

dirigible   Describes an aerostat which can be directed or steered. That is, a balloon which is propelled and directed by machine. Envelopes of a dirigible may be rigid or nonrigid, but are usually more shaped like a cigar. See **blimp.**

downwind   Unlike other aircraft, balloons take off and land downwind—which means traveling in the same direction as the wind.

drag line   A long, usually heavy rope that in earlier times was dangled from the gondola of gas balloons to help regulate altitude during low-level flight by acting as regulating ballast. Not usually found in hot-air balloons.

drift   A movement away from a selected flight path, caused by the wind. The term is sometimes used when the wind doesn't behave as forecast, and your balloon "drifts" from the tentative course you had plotted on your chart.

dumping-type balloon   A type of balloon in which deflation is obtained by releasing the throat of the balloon while the crown is secured by the crown line, q.v. The balloon envelope inverts as the hot air seeks to escape. Rip seams at the throat end of the balloon assist in the speedy evacuation of hot air from the envelope. See also **ripping balloon.**

envelope   The fabric part of a balloon, which contains either gas or hot air. It is made of gores of specially woven and proof-stressed synthetic material.

Federal Aviation Administration   An administration within the Department of Transportation with the duty to foster aviation and the responsibility of supervising, regulating and administering aviation.

flight valve   See **cruise valve.**

footropes   Term formerly used for suspension wires or lines.

forced landing   Landing an aircraft because you have no other options—such as when you've run out of fuel. A *precautionary landing*, in which the pilot elects to land rather than continue the flight for some reason, is not a forced landing, which normally implies circumstances beyond the pilot's control.

gondola   also **basket,** and formerly *car*—especially in early dirigibles.

The classical wicker basket which is suffering replacement by aluminum section or fiberglass, from which the balloon is controlled by the pilot. Wicker is much kinder to humans on rough landings than modern counterparts, having greater ability to cushion shock.

ground inflator, blower, also **cold inflator, blower**   A gasoline- or electric-powered fan, usually a cage-type blower, used for preliminary ground inflation instead of flapping the envelope full of cold air—which takes much longer.

ground speed   The speed of a flying machine in relation to the ground over which it is flying. Ground speed relates to distance traveled over the ground. Air speed relates to speed relative to the air through which the aircraft is flying.

A hot-air or free balloon only has ground speed, since it travels with the wind. A blimp or rigid airship which is powered has both ground and air speed.

landing   Returning a flying machine to the ground, in a controlled manner and bringing it to a stop.

load tapes   Special load-bearing tapes sewn over the seams of the balloon and running from crown to mouth, where they connect with the suspension wires, or **footropes.** The tapes help distribute the load evenly over the surface of the balloon.

loft   A technical term to describe what happens in a hard landing, when the balloon snaps the gondola back into the air in a bounce-type motion. This is called *lofting.*

Also refers to an upper room where sails and sometimes balloons are made —as in Balloon Loft.

logbook   A pilot's record of flights made.

maneuvering vent   A self-sealing aperture which permits for the discrete outlet of hot air to check an ascent or to initiate a descent. It is controlled by a line to the gondola.

metering valve   See **cruise valve.**

north pole   Crown, or **apex,** of balloon envelope.

preflight, preflight inspection   The inspection conducted on the ground by the pilot-in-command of a flying machine prior to any flight.

pyrometer   A thermocouple used to measure the temperature of the hot air in the upper section of a hot-air balloon. A temperature gauge in the gondola relays this information to the pilot; this data in turn may be compared with the outside air temperature—if such a gauge is carried—to determine temperature differential. There is usually a "red line" temperature which must not be exceeded; this is normally 250°F or 300°F and may only be used for up to ten minutes before the fabric is seriously weakened. See also **telltales.**

regulator, regulator valve   See **cruise valve.**

rip line, rip cord, release cord   A line from the ripping panel which leads to the gondola. The last six feet or so of the rip line are made of bright red fabric or line as a visual warning that it is not to be used except when needed. A healthy tug of the rip line opens the ripping panel, permitting the hot air to escape, thus deflating the envelope.

Also used to describe the line which opens the rip seams in dumping balloons.

ripping balloon   A balloon which deflates by ripping open a large area—ripping panel—at the crown of the envelope. See also **dumping balloon.**

rip seam   Special seams at the throat of dumping balloons which are opened just prior to deflation by pulling a release—or rip—cord.

skirt   Most hot-air balloons now use a special section of material beneath the throat to shroud the area around the burner once inflation is completed, in the interests of fuel efficiency. The skirt may be part of the envelope or not. What it does is reduce loss of burner heat by gusts of wind across the throat.

solo   Flying with only the pilot aboard the craft. Specifically refers to a student pilot's first flight on his own.

suspension wires, lines (cables)   Flexible, stainless (usually), heat-resisting steel cables which suspend the gondola beneath the envelope and connect with the load tapes. Also still known as **footropes.**

telltale   Special pieces of heat-sensitive material placed within the top of a hot-air balloon to provide warning when temperatures have been developed that have likely caused damage to the envelope material. They are set in a small cage with temperatures marked according to manufacturers' specifications.

temperature differential   The difference between the captive air inside the envelope of a hot-air balloon and the outside air temperature. Average differential required for flight is between 70°F and 90°F, depending on air density.

temperature red line   Maximum safe operating temperature of the air within a hot-air balloon. Depending on the type of material used, this ranges from around 250°F to 350°F. Each maker has a specification—*You should know the operating temperature parameters of each balloon you fly.*

tether, tether line   An anchor line used during training or for a captive balloon flight, in no- or low-wind conditions. Tethers were used extensively in earlier times for making observation, especially in military events, such as the Civil War. Tethered balloons known as *barrage balloons* were used in Britain during World War II to discourage low-level attack by German bomber command. They were quite successful.

thermal aerostat   Fancy way of talking about a hot-air balloon.

touch-and-go   Refers to a regimen in which a student pilot makes a series of takeoffs and landings without coming to a full stop. The landing is not completed before a new ascent is initiated—save for the final landing.

variometer   A sensitive vertical speed indicator, which measures the relative up and down movement of a flying machine in the air. Variometers are used mostly by balloon and glider pilots.

VSI, Vertical Speed Indicator   An instrument to tell at what rate you are climbing or descending. A little bit slow in presenting the actual rate, the VSI will nevertheless tell you immediately in which direction you are moving. Variometers, q.v., are speedier.

weigh off, weigh   Adopted from maritime usage (weigh anchor), to weigh off refers to an ascent which is gradual, in that a balloon drifts gently upward with only a few pounds of buoyancy. Term probably started with gas balloons when ground ballast was removed to provide positive buoyancy.

Bibliography
and Suggested Reading

Because ballooning is a relatively old activity, and somewhat international in origin, this reading list is quite different from most. A great deal of material written at the time ballooning originated is still available to the keen student and diligent researcher. And so this list has titles going back to those early days, including special-interest books in French, German and Italian, in addition to English. Where translations into English are available, these have been listed with a reference to the original text.

Specific instruction books are few and far between, although some of the best currently available are put out by Wind Drifters Balloon Club, 1459 North Irving Avenue, Glendale, California, 91209.

Ambers, Henry J. *The Dirigible and the Future*. Brooklyn, N.Y.: Theo Gaus' Sons, Inc., 1970.

Amik, M. L. *History of Donaldson's Balloon Ascensions*. Cincinnati: Cincinnati News Co., 1875.

Andrée, Salomon August. *The Andrée Diaries*. Translated from the Swedish by Edward Adams-Ray. London: John Lane, 1931.

Bacon, Gertrude. *The Record of an Aeronaut; The Life of John M. Bacon by his Daughter*. Haymarket, London: John Lang, 1907.

Baldwin, Munson. *With Brass and Gas*. Boston: Beacon Press, 1967.

Baldwin, Thomas. *Airopaida*. Chester, 1786.

Beauchamp, Baron Selle de. *Extrait des Mémoires d'un officier des aérostiers aux armées de 1793 à 1799*. Paris, 1853.

Blanchard, Jean-Pierre. *The First Air Voyage in America*. Facsimile reprinting of "My Forty-Fifth Ascension and the First in America." Philadelphia: Penn Mutual Life Insurance Co., 1943.

Blanchard, Jean-Pierre. *Relation de la quatorzième ascension de Blanchard*. Lille, 1789.

Block, Eugene B. *Above the Civil War*. Howell-North, 1966.

Boesman, Dr. J. *Luchtschepen en Ballons*. Alkmar, Holland: De Alkenreeks.

Bois, William Pene du. *The 21 Balloons*. London: Robert Hale Ltd., 1949.

Broke-Smith, Brig. P. W. L. *The History of Early British Military Aeronautics*. London: Royal Engineers Journal, 1952.

Brewer, Griffiths. *Ballooning and Kite Ballooning*. Air League of the British Empire, 1940.

Cameron, D. A. *Hot Air Ballooning Operating Handbook*. Bristol, England: Cameron Balloons Ltd.

Cavallo, Tiberius. *The History and Practice of Aerostation*. London: Cavallo, 1785.

Charles, Jacques Alexandre. *Relation du voyage aérostatique de Charles*. Paris, 1783.

Clarke, Basil. *The History of Airships*. London: Herbert Jenkins, 1961.

Cornish, Joseph Jenkins III. *The Air Arm of the Confederacy*. Richmond, Virginia: Richmond Civil War Centennial Committee, 1963.

Coxwell, Henry. *My Life and Balloon Experiences*. 2 vols. London: A. H. Allen, 1887–89.

Degan, Jakob. *Beschreibung einer neuen Flugmaschine*. Wien, 1808.

Delacombe, Harry. *The Boys' Book of Airships*. London: Grant Richards, 1910.

Dixon, Peter L. with Jay Fiondella. *Ballooning*. New York: Ballantine Books, 1972.

Dolfus, Charles. *Balloons*. London: Prentice Hall International, 1962.

Dolfus, Charles. *Les Ballons*. Paris, 1960.

Dolfus, Charles and H. Bouche. *Histoire de l'Aéronautique*. Revised edition. Paris, 1942.

Douty, Esther M. *Ball in the Sky*. New York: Henry Holt & Co., 1956.

Easterby, J. H. "Confederate Silk Dress Balloon." *Historical & Genealogical Magazine*, Vol. XLV (1944).

Eckener, Hugo. *My Zeppelins*. London: Putnam, 1958.

Eiloart, Arnold. *Flight of the Small World*. London: Hodder & Stoughton, 1959.

Faroux, C. and C. Bonnet, eds. *Aéro-Manuel*. Paris: Dinot & Pinat, 1914.

Fisher, John. *Airlift 1870*. London: Max Parrish, 1965.

Fonvielle, W. de. *Adventures in the Air*. Translated by J. S. Keltie. London: Edward Stanford, 1877.

Forster, T. *Annals of some remarkable aerial and alpine voyages*. London, 1832.

Fritsche, Carl B. *The Metalclad Airship*. London: Royal Aeronautical Society, 1931.

Gardiner, Leslie. *Man in the Clouds*. London: W. R. Chambers Ltd., 1963.

Garnerin, Elisa. *Ascensione aerostatica da Madamigella Garnerin*. Milan, 1824.

Gibbs-Smith, Charles. *A History of Flying*. London: Batsford, 1953.

Glaisher, James with Camille Flammarion and Gaston Tissandier. *Travels in the Air*. London: Richard Bentley, 1871. (Originally published as *Voyages Aeriens*, Paris, 1870.)

Glines, Lt. Col. C. V., USAF, ed. *Lighter-than-air Flight*. New York: Franklin Watts, Inc. for The Watts Aerospace Library.

Grieder, Karl. *Zeppeline Giganten der Lufte*. Zurich: Orell Fussli Verlag.

Hall, George Eli. *A Balloon Ascension at Midnight*. San Francisco: Paul Elder and Morgan, 1902.

Haydon, F. Stansbury. *Aeronautics in the Union and Confederate Armies*. Baltimore: Johns Hopkins Press, 1941.

Higham, Robin. *The British Rigid Airship 1908–31*. London: G. J. Foulis & Co., 1968.

Hildebrandt, A. *Airships Past and Present*. Translated by W. H. Story. London: Constable, 1908. (Originally published as *Die Luftschiffahrt nach ihrer geschichtlichen und gegenwaertigen*, Entwicklung; München, 1907).

Hodgson, J. E. *The History of Aeronautics in Great Britain*. London: Oxford University Press, 1924.

Hogg, Garry. *Airship Over the Pole*. New York: Abelard, 1969.

Jackson, Robert. *Airships in Peace and War*. London: Cassell, 1971.

Kirschner, E. J. *The Zeppelin in the Atomic Age*. Urbana, Illinois: University of Illinois Press, 1957.

Lamorisse, Albert. *Trip in a Balloon*. New York: Doubleday & Co., 1960.

Lausanne, Edita, producer. *The Romance of Ballooning*. New York: The Viking Press, a Studio Book, 1971.

Leasor, James. *The Millionth Chance* (Story of R–101), London: Hamish Hamilton, 1957.

Lunardi, V. *An account of five aerial voyages in Scotland*. London, 1786.

———. *An account of the first aerial voyage in England*. London, 1784.

Mabley, Edward. *Motor Balloon America: First Try at Atlantic Air Crossing*. Greene, 1965.

Marion, F. *Wonderful Balloon Ascents*. London: Cassell, Petter & Galpin, 1870. (Originally published as *Les Ballons et Les Voyages aériens*. Paris, 1867.)

Mason, Thomas Monck. *Account of the late aeronautical expedition from London to Weilburg*. London, 1836.

———. *Aeronautica*. London: Westley, 1838.

Milbank, Jeremiah Jr. *First Century of Flight in America*. Princeton, New Jersey: Princeton University Press, 1943.

Military Ballooning, 1862. Three papers reprinted from the Professional Aviation Press, Edgware, Middlesex, England, 1967.

Miller, Francis Trevelyan. *The World in the Air*. New York: G. P. Putnam's Sons, 1930.

Monk, F. V. and H. J. Winter. *Adventure Above the Clouds*. London: Blackie & Son Ltd., 1943.

Montgolfier, Joseph de. *Discours prononcé à l'Académie des sciences de Lyon*. Paris, 1784.

Mooney, Michael M. *The Hindenburg*. New York: Bantam, 1973.

Morse, Francis. "The Nuclear Airship." *New Scientist*, July 4, 1966.

Nader, Felix. *À Terre et en l'air . . . Mémoires du Géant*. Paris, 1864.

———. *Les Ballons en 1870. Ce qu'on aurait pu faire; ce qu'on à fait*. Paris, 1870.

Norgaard, Erik. *The Book of Balloons*. New York: Crown, 1972.

Piccard, Auguste. *Au-dessus des nuages*. Paris, 1933.

Piccard, Joan Russell. *Adventure on the Wind*. Los Angeles: Nash Publishing, 1971.

Rolt, L. T. C. *The Aeronauts: A History of Balloons 1783–1903*. New York: Walker & Co., 1966.

Royal Engineers. *Military Ballooning 1862*. Reprint of three papers by Aviation Press, Edgware, Middlesex, England, 1967.

Rozier, F. Pilâtre de. *La Vie et les Mémoires de Pilâtre de Rozier*. Paris, 1786.
———. *Première expérience de la Montgolfière construite par ordre du Roi*. Paris, 1784.
Sadler, James. *Aerial Voyage of Messrs. Sadler & Clayfield*. Bristol: A. Brown, 1810.
———. *Authentic Narrative of Mr. Sadler Across the Irish Channel*. Dublin: Tyrell, 1812.
Sage, Mrs. L. A. *A letter addressed to a female friend*. London, 1785.
Santos-Dumont, Alberto. *My Airships*. London: Grant Richards, 1904.
Savini, Savino. *Notizie biografiche del conte Francesco Zambeccari Bolognese*. Turin, Italy, 1847.
Scott, G. H. *Handling and Mooring of Airships* (R–38 Memorial Lecture, 1929): Royal Aeronautical Society, London.
Seibel, Dr. C. W. *Helium—Child of the Sun*. Lawrence, Kansas: University Press of Kansas, 1968.
Shute, Nevil. *Slide Rule*. London: Wm. Heinemann Ltd., 1954.
Sims, Lydel. *Thaddeus Lowe: Uncle Sam's First Airman*. New York: G. P. Putnam's Sons, 1964.
Sinclair, J. A. *Airships in Peace and War*. London: Rich & Cowan, 1934.
———. *Famous Airships of the World*. London: Frederick Muller Ltd., 1959.
Smith, Anthony. *JAMBO: African Balloon Safari*. New York: E. P. Dutton, 1963. (Also published in paperback by Signet, 1965.)
Smith, Anthony. *Throw Out Two Hands*. London: Allen & Unwin Ltd., 1963.
Smith, Richard K. *The Airships Akron and Macon*. Annapolis, Maryland: Naval Institute Press, 1965.
Stehling, Kurt R. and William Beller. *Skyhooks*. New York: Doubleday, 1962.
Sundman, Per-Olof. *The Flight of the Eagle*. New York: Pantheon, 1970.
Supf, Peter. *Das Buch der deutschen Fluggeschichte*. Berlin, 1935.
Tissandier, Gaston. *Histoire de mes ascensions*. Paris, 1888.
———. *Histoire des ballons et des aéronautes célèbres*. 2 vols. Paris, 1887–90.
Trykare, Tre and John W. R. Taylor. *The Lore of Flight*. New York: Time-Life Books.
Turnbull, Christine. *Hot Air Ballooning*. London: Speed and Sports Publications, 1970.
Turnor, Hatton. *Astra Castra, Experiment and Adventures in the Atmosphere*. London: Chapman & Hall, 1865.
Verne, Jules. *Five Weeks in a Balloon, or Journeys and Discoveries in Africa by Three Englishmen*. New York: Hurst & Co., 1869.
Williams, T. B. (Captain Bill), A.F.C. *Airship Pilot No. 28*. London: William Kimber, 1974.
Wind Drifters Balloon Club. *Examination Guide*.
———. *Flight Curriculum*.
———. *Introduction to Club Ballooning*.
———. *Training Manual*.
Wise, John. *A System of Aeronautics*. Philadelphia, 1850.
———. *Through the Air*. Arno, 1971 reprint of 1873 edition.
Wykeham, Peter. *Santos-Dumont; a study in Obsession*. London: Putnam, 1962.

Zambeccari, **F.** *Descrizione della machina aerostatica del cittadina Francesco Zambeccari.* Bologna, Italy, 1803.

Magazines

Ballooning. Journal of the Balloon Federation of America. Published quarterly on the 15th of January, April, July and October. Editorial Offices: 2516 Hiawatha Drive, N.E., Albuquerque, New Mexico 87112.

Aerostat. Bimonthly Journal of the British Balloon and Airship Club. Write to: C. Redhead, BBAC Membership Secretary, 4 Goodways Drive, Bracknell, Berkshire, England RG12 3AU.

Index